Twayne's English Authors Series

EDITOR OF THIS VOLUME

Arthur F. Kinney

University of Massachusetts, Amherst

Fulke Greville

TEAS 302

Reproduced by courtesy of Lord Willoughby de Broke

Fulke Greville

FULKE GREVILLE

By Charles Larson

University of Missouri, St. Louis

TWAYNE PUBLISHERS

A DIVISION OF G. K. HALL & CO., BOSTON

Copyright © 1980 by G. K. Hall & Co.

Published in 1980 by Twayne Publishers,
A Division of G. K. Hall & Co.
All Rights Reserved

Printed on permanent/durable acid-free paper and bound
in the United States of America

First Printing

Library of Congress Cataloging in Publication Data

Larson, Charles Howard.
Fulke Greville.

(Twayne's English authors series ; TEAS 302)
Bibliography: p. 142
Includes index.
1. Brooke, Fulke Grevelle, Baron, 1554–1628—
Criticism and interpretation.
PR2216.L3   1980   821'.3   80-14636
ISBN 0-8057-6794-0

Contents

About The Author

Charles Larson received his B.A. in 1966 from Carleton College. Under the auspices of a Woodrow Wilson Dissertation Fellowship, he earned his Ph.D. in 1970 from Indiana University. Since 1970, he has been a professor in the English department of the University of Missouri, St. Louis specializing in non-dramatic literature of the English Renaissance. Having held the position of Director of Graduate Studies, he is presently departmental chairman. Dr. Larson has received grants from the University of Missouri, St. Louis and the Henry E. Huntington Library and has published principally in the areas of Elizabethan prose fiction and poetry and prose of the period of the English Civil War.

Editor's Foreword

Charles Larson's study of Fulke Greville shows how a successful court politician managed to write a small but impressive body of original poetry that often challenged the ideas and policies of the very courts he served. Concentrating on the literary works, Larson demonstrates the important if uneven achievement of a Renaissance poet whose work has only recently been studied seriously by examining in detail how Greville transformed the sonnet cycle from lyric love poetry to philosophic statement and how, in the *Life of Sidney,* he changed the occasion for simple panegyric into an apology and critique that serves political and religious ends. Greville emerges here as a man who sought religious serenity all his life but died unable to find evidence that God would favor him, yet remained stubbornly unwilling to give himself over to religious despair.

Arthur F. Kinney

Preface

The literary reputation of Fulke Greville, First Baron Brooke, has been largely a creation of the twentieth century. His writing was known only to a small number of his contemporaries, and awareness of his work dwindled still further during the eighteenth and nineteenth centuries. When he was edited by the indefatigable Alexander Grosart at the end of the last century, he had all but disappeared from sight. Grosart served Greville in the same way that his editions served several other Renaissance authors, and Greville came to be recognized during the next several decades as an important voice in Elizabethan lyric poetry.

Not until the last ten years, however, has Greville's achievement in genres other than the lyric come to be much noted, nor have many details of his life been made available to modern students of the literature of the period. Now, equipped with good texts for most of the works and fortified by two biographies, we are in a position to undertake an examination of his literary merit that will eventually, I am sure, establish him as one of the most versatile and profound artists of his exceptionally rich era.

The present study endeavors to present a general critical survey and assessment of Greville's literary production. I have not attempted to redo the biographical spadework so ably performed recently by Ronald Rebholz and Joan Rees, though I have occasionally differed from some of the conclusions that they have drawn from their research. On the other hand, I have attempted what neither of them professes to aim at: an aesthetic consideration of all of Greville's works. To thus pay attention to everything does not, of course, suggest a judgment of equality of achievement in those works, and I trust that my opinions on their relative merits will emerge with sufficient clarity.

Following a chapter of historical and biographical introduction, I take up the works in chapters that are certainly generic in their organization and that may be chronological as well. The "may" is necessary here since, as will be seen, the exact order and dating of Greville's writings and revisions remain issues of considerable indeterminacy. Thus, I cannot be certain that the chronological progression from one genre to another which my arrangement of chapters sometimes implies is in fact correct, but there is considerable justification for thinking that it is, for understanding Greville's literary energy as being essentially of the sort that turned from one form to another in search of expressive vehicles for his themes.

It is my hope that the totality of this study will elucidate those themes and will show Greville to be the kind of writer whose achievement, although not well known to his contemporaries, furnishes an example of what his age professed to value so highly: earnestness and depth of thought coupled with inventiveness in form and technique. That these works should have come from a social grandee who saw his long life as devoted principally to government service makes them remarkable testaments to the actual existence of the ideal to which we sometimes give the name of the Renaissance man.

CHARLES LARSON

University of Missouri, St. Louis

Chronology

1628   Greville fatally stabbed by a servant and dies in London on 30 September. Buried in St. Mary's Church, Warwick.

1633   *Certain Learned and Elegant Works of Fulke, Lord Brooke* published.

CHAPTER 1

The Courtier

I *Child of "A Hard Stepmother to Poets"*

PHILIP Sidney, writing around 1581, identified a national need "to inquire why England, the mother of excellent minds, should be grown so hard a stepmother to poets."[1] The anemic condition of English letters in the 1570s and 1580s was clearly a matter of considerable concern to Sidney, and, in the too-brief time that remained in his life, he worked earnestly, if intermittently, to improve matters. His interest in the situation was presumably shared by his close friend Fulke Greville, who by this point had also been writing poetry for several years. The surprising element in this for the modern student of Renaissance literature is that, having made this observation, neither Sidney nor Greville went on to give imaginative literature higher priority in his affairs than he did. During the years that immediately preceded and followed the *Defence of Poesie*, both young men were mainly preoccupied with advancing their careers as politicians and courtiers, with literature placing a distant second in their activities.

This important indication of the relative value attached to literature by individuals of Sidney's and Greville's talents and class suggests that they would perhaps have been quite surprised to learn that their reputations for posterity were to be based upon their nongovernmental efforts. The literature of the two decades could certainly have used the enrichment that still more extensive labors from Greville and Sidney would have given it, one of the ironies of the period being that it was not until after Sidney's death that English poetry and fiction began to flourish. The authors' reluctance to commit more of their energies to the creation of literature is thus characteristic of the pattern to be discerned in the attributes and values of the Elizabethan era as a whole.

That the period did not encourage its cerebral young men to go in literary directions is perhaps understandable in view of the novelty of the national situation during the first half of Elizabeth's reign. With the welcome arrival of a considerable measure of political and religious stability after the Settlement of 1559, the nation found itself in a position to bring into a productive focus the governmental energies that had been scattered in various directions during the previous decades of political uncertainty. Unlike her father Henry VIII, the last of the roving kings to believe that his entire realm could be governed personally, Elizabeth conceived of the monarchy in organizational terms, thus giving England a rudimentary bureaucracy in which men saw numerous openings for advancement through application of merit and flattery. The possibility for government service could only have been welcomed by those who, like Greville and Sidney, saw such careers as proper and desirable ways of participating in the future of a nation that seemed to them destined to become one of the great powers of Europe. The sense of expansive optimism that so permeated the 1560s and 1570s had not yet produced the condition of competitive intrigue that was to succeed it, and so an aristocrat could feel that his personal fulfillment and the fulfillment of his nation were happily congruent.

Greville was no different from other young men born into affluence and social position in wanting to be close to the source of national power, but he turned out to be a good deal more successful than most of them in arriving at and remaining in proximity to it. There was, to be sure, a decade of forced retirement at the start of James I's reign, but, apart from that, Greville displayed remarkable political tenacity and longevity. It could be said (and has been) that Greville's interest in power was so great that he was willing to make any compromise of principle to insure the preservation of his status. There is some truth to this, although it would be going too far to extend the generalization into an accusation of political spinelessness. Greville may have found his thinking at variance with that of other courtiers, but rarely did he differ in a fundamental way with the positions of the two monarchs whom he served. By nature conservative, always seeking to maintain social stability by avoiding disruption, he, as this book's survey of his writings will show, committed himself to the cause of protestant royalism so thoroughly that it is not particularly to the point to wonder about his political flexibililty. Even during the years when he was out of favor, a period of time when he came to despise particular corruptions of the royal court, there is no sign of his wavering from his general belief in royalism. Indeed, some of the most articulate defenses of royal prerogative were written during this period. In this, he differs from Sidney, since recent interpretations of Sidney's career have identified a recurring sense of frustration as a dominant trait in both his life and his literature. Prevented by Elizabeth from assuming the active role that he desired for himself, Sidney retired to write fiction and poetry that, by imaginative analogue, displays and analyzes the frustrations inherent in his views on the topics of sovereignty and obedience.[2] If Greville ever chafed under the royal curb in a similar way, he kept his irritation far better hidden than did his friend. He was content to bide his time, to think, to write, and to wait.

II   *The Two Careers of the Courtier*

There are few, if any, surprises in an examination of Greville's early life. His family background prepared him for prominence, and he seems never to have shied from his privileged responsibilities. His father, also named Fulke, was a prosperous Warwickshire landowner, and his mother, born Anne Neville, was from one of the wealthiest families of the sixteenth century. The years between his birth on 3 October 1654, and his entrance into Shrewsbury grammar school at the age of ten in the company of Philip Sidney are largely unaccounted for. The reasons for his father's sending him the relatively long distance to Shrewsbury are similarly unclear, although Ronald Rebholz, Greville's most complete and definitive biographer, suggests that it may have been that Greville's father and Sidney's father, who is known to have had business in Shrewsbury, thought that it would be good for the boys to stay together to keep one another company.[3]

Greville and Sidney were schoolmates for about four years at Shrewsbury until they left to matriculate at the university, Sidney at Oxford and Greville at Cambridge. Rebholz points out that the familial decision to send Greville to the university is indicative of new attitudes on the part of the gentry and nobility toward the universities. Once ignored as essentially irrelevant to the practical tasks of managing estates, the universities now began exerting a greater appeal to the gentry who, under the prodding of human-

ists such as Erasmus, More, and Elyot, were coming to believe it
to be advantageous to give their sons more education than they
had previously thought necessary.[4]

The curriculum that Greville would have followed at Cambridge had indeed very few, if any, practical aspects to it. Still
largely derived from the medieval curriculum, the reading would
have been confined almost entirely to the Latin classics. Cicero
(who had doubtless also been a focal point of the study at Shrewsbury), Quintilian, Pliny, Aristotle, and Plato in the original
Greek—these would have been the authors more or less mastered
by Greville in lectures and tutorials during his university years.
There was probably very little in the program of study that was
specifically literary, but the training in logic and rhetoric (albeit
Latin rhetoric) was not totally inappropriate for someone who
was pointing himself toward a life of government service.

Greville was reunited with Sidney in the late 1570s when they
both were introduced to Elizabeth's court by Sidney's father.
That court, a large and politically sensitive body of officeholders
and office aspirants, could presumably have sustained someone in
its midst at a low rank almost indefinitely. Such stasis was not
common, however, inasmuch as men coming to court were usually ambitious by nature and little given to interest in unlucra-
tive positions: like Greville, they were often giving up opportunities to operate family landholdings. Advancement at court
usually came about through the patronage of one or another faction into which the body as a whole divided itself, and thus the
faction to which one belonged made at least as much difference as
the strength of one's personal qualities. Greville and Sidney both
aligned themselves at once with the party of Robert Dudley, the
earl of Leicester, Sidney's uncle and an old friend of the Greville
family. Although the choice may have been an inevitable one, it
was in most regards not the most personally advantageous. Leicester's faction embraced and advocated a radical variety of
protestantism which held all matters of national policy to be good
or bad to the extent that they advanced the protestant cause. It
was an extreme view, and Elizabeth liked by nature to avoid ex-
tremes, preferring to play one faction off against another and
pick a middle way. Greville received a number of minor duties
and offices from the queen, but in the main his progress was
retarded. Sidney sought escape from the frustration by leading a
campaign to the Low Countries, only to die a hero's death. Gre-

ville remained behind in England, alive, in mourning for his friend, and apparently still negotiating his own rise through the bureaucracy.

By 1594 Greville had formed a close association with Robert Devereux, the earl of Essex, Sidney's political heir and an increasing favorite of Elizabeth. Essex had taken over the leadership of the radical protestant faction after the deaths of Leicester and Sidney and was now leading the opposition to the faction headed by William Cecil, Baron Burghley, and his son Robert, a man who was to prove to be Greville's greatest antagonist a few years later. It was as a friend of Essex that Greville at last achieved in 1598 a major office, that of the treasurer of the Navy, and it was surely as a friend of Essex that Greville must have thought he had reached his political demise when in 1601 Essex revolted and was executed for treason. Oddly, however, Elizabeth continued to favor Greville and he had expectations of appointment to the Privy Council when the queen aborted his plans with her death in 1603.

Robert Cecil had assiduously worked to insure his own transition from Elizabeth to her successor James, a transition so successful for him that he found himself with strong new authority under the new monarch. He set about eliminating rivals, and Greville, as a member of the opposing party and as an obviously astute politician, was one of the first to go. Losing the treasurership of the Navy, barely holding on to other lesser offices, finding himself with no access to the king, Greville had little choice but to retreat to Warwick Castle in 1604 to begin a decade-long period of rumination and writing. The literature created during this period is, as shall be shown, extensive in its variety but characterized throughout by a disillusionment with the ways of men and their institutions and a turn toward the hope of divine grace.

That Greville had, however, not lost all interest in worldly matters is shown by the alacrity with which he moved to reestablish himself at court upon Cecil's death in 1612. Displaying as much adroitness as ever, he had arranged by 1614 to have himself named chancellor and under-treasurer of the Exchequer and privy councillor. As Rebholz so succinctly phrases it: "his second career had begun."[5]

The shape of this second career bears strong resemblances to that of the first. His actions in the Exchequer were those of a man who believed that governments could achieve certain desirable

ends but who was also greatly interested in advancing his own
cause. The extent to which this self-serving attitude contradicts
the otherworldly aims of the literature that he was writing and
revising at this time will be a subject to which this study will
return later. During his years in the Exchequer, Greville manifested a political malleability that F. J. Levy finds to be
characteristic of the generation of aggressive politicians who had
entered government service in the second half of Elizabeth's
reign:

Since many of them, as convinced Protestants, saw state service as a kind
of moral duty and as an opportunity to steer policy toward the assistance
of the reformed religion anywhere in Europe, their exclusion from important political posts was peculiarly frustrating. That political failure,
coupled with the shock, first of Sidney's death, then of Essex's, scarred all
of them. By the time the survivors returned to politics, they were prepared
to be very pliant politicians indeed—as they had need to be in the new
courtier world of a still younger generation represented by [James' new
favorite] Buckingham.[6]

There is no record of any real dissent entered by Greville to the
sometimes bizarre policies of James and Buckingham during these
years. The story, as Rebholz presents it, is one of a man who was
grateful for meaningful work and who did not mind dirtying his
hands in the corruption of the Jacobean court in order to carry
out that work. No accusations of important malfeasance have
ever been brought against Greville, but he was certainly quiet
while his superior the lord treasurer, the earl of Suffolk, lined his
pockets with government funds.[7]

In 1621, an old and feeble man, Greville lost his Exchequer
office, though his long and faithful tenure was rewarded with a
barony. He stayed on at court during his final years, how much
out of habit and how much out of a sense of purposeful loyalty
cannot be very accurately determined. He survived King James
by three years, but his service to Charles was minimal indeed.
Having lived to the age of seventy-three, he died, ironically, of
unnatural causes. A servant who seems to have felt that he had
been inadequately provided for in a will that Greville had just
prepared stabbed him one day as he was helping Greville dress.
The wound was not immediately fatal, and he lingered on for a
month. He had given orders that the escaped assailant not be pur-

sued, "desiring that not any man should lose his life for him."[8]
Caring little about living, he seems at last to have reached that
state of *contemptu mundi* that he had so long praised in his
writing. He was buried in Warwick in a tomb that he had
ordered built with an inscription that summed up what he saw as
the dominant features of his existence:

Fulke Greville
Servant to Queen Elizabeth
Councillor to King James
And Friend to Sir Philip Sidney
Trophaeum Peccati

That, after three distinctions of which he or any man could be
deservedly proud, he should still choose to label himself a "trophy
of sin" says much about his perception of the value of his life. He
had not helped the world, but, then, the world was perhaps
beyond help. He had not helped himself, for he probably felt the
weight of his own iniquity to be heavier now than he had fifty
years earlier. He could only hope that somehow sin's trophy could
yet be transmuted into the crown of divine grace.

III   *Greville's Development as a Man of Letters*

When he was fifty-eight years old Greville wrote to Sir John
Coke, telling him, among other things, that "I know the world
and believe in God." Although he probably intended for the
statement to be applied only to his attitude toward the business of
living, the polarity indicated here says much about the dual
nature of the sources of inspiration for his literature. Always a
man of the world, Greville's writing reflected various versions of
that world, though, as the years went by, he came increasingly to
reject the allure of the mundane for the holy presence that had existed implicitly even in his earliest poetry. To express and analyze
this dualism, Greville chose to work in literary forms—the lyric,
the rhetorical tragedy, the discursive philosophical poem—that
were, by and large, traditional and familiar to his contemporaries. Contenting himself with a minimum of formal innova-
tion, he invested most of his artistic energy in the process of
thematic development, in the display of the workings of a mind
whose capacity for moral insight and generalization had few, if

any, equals among Renaissance authors. Unfortunately, however, this intellectual achievement did not consistently find an outlet in the striking and memorable diction and imagery of great poetry. At his best, he combined thought and technique in a way unsurpassed by any of his contemporaries. One can only feel a sense of loss at the realization that these greater moments did not come to Greville more frequently than they did.

His conformity to contemporary modes is perhaps most noticeable to the modern reader at the start of his career, a point at which he seems to have decided rather self-consciously to become a sonneteer. He was never quite as at home with the love sonnet as was Sidney, however, and, as the next chapter will show, before long he began introducing nontraditional elements into the content of the short love lyric. More interested in the effects of love on man as a social creature than he was on any elaboration of the pure passion in relative isolation, Greville came to turn the lyric form into a vehicle for examining man's attitudes toward his culture and his destiny rather than always toward his lover.

When, in the last third of the *Caelica* cycle of lyrics, he began taking religion as the overt and principal subject of his poetry, he was departing even more significantly from contemporary poetic norms. The history of the religious lyric in the sixteenth century is not a particularly rich one, and, consequently, Greville had few models for these poems. More to his taste, in any case, than were the love sonnets, the religious lyrics afforded him the opportunity for a spiritual introspection that possessed simultaneously both intimacy and wider applicability. Probably written a few years prior to Donne's *Holy Sonnets*, Greville's poems anticipate much that is best about the seventeenth-century meditative lyric. That they have not received their share of critical acclaim is by now a long-standing injustice.

Given this diversity of subject matter and far-reaching evolution of attitudes, it is not surprising that the unity of the *Caelica* sequence has been questioned. Geoffrey Bullough, whose edition of *Caelica* and the plays is deserving of so much tribute, perhaps epitomizes the reactions of many readers of *Caelica* when he asserts that there is no real principle of unity in the sequence but rather that it is the "repository of all those of his shorter pieces which he wished to survive."[9] More recently, however, critics such as Richard Waswo and Norman K. Farmer, Jr. have argued for the presence of a much greater degree of structural unity and integrity in the *Caelica* poems.[10] Farmer thinks that, in spite of their widespread dates of composition, Greville's poems were eventually brought together by their author with the intention that they cohere thematically and that *Caelica* is not so different after all from other Renaissance sonnet cycles where there are unifying themes that underlie variation in symbols and subjects.[11]

The fact that Greville did choose to bring them together, that he did choose to have them copied out in a sequence by an amanuensis points toward another feature of his achievement deserving of notice: his apparently almost compulsive habit of revision. Few authors of his era displayed such a reluctance to consider anything ever to be in its final form. It seems likely that Greville kept his manuscripts in an almost constant state of revision, a practice that has made the job of his modern editors an unenviable one. In some instances, as with his drama *Alaham*, for example, it can be established that versions of the play once existed that are no longer extant,[12] while in other cases, such as the *Life of Sir Philip Sidney*, the modern scholar has no fewer than four different texts apparently written at various points over a period of several years. Even in the instance of *Caelica*, once a scribe had assembled and copied the collection of lyrics the author came back to them, to some of them several times, for later changes. Farmer notes that the evidence of the Warwick Castle manuscript shows that Greville not only corrected about half of the total number of lyrics but also seems to have had further afterthoughts about their placement, or even their inclusion in the manuscript.[13] Like Yeats, Greville must have felt that poems written at one point in his experience could be, indeed needed to be, revised to reflect changed perspectives on that experience. In this situation, all of a poet's works undergo a constant process of accretive growth, usually in size and always in texture.

Even if Greville had managed to put his works into a form that could have seemed to him conclusive, it is doubtful that many of them would have been presented by him for publication. Always thinking of himself as a courtier and a statesman rather than as a writer, he placed himself in the Renaissance tradition of the gentleman amateur for whom publication would have been demeaning. There was a pirated edition of his play *Mustapha* in 1609, but otherwise nothing that he wrote appeared in print during his lifetime. In 1633, five years after his death, the greater

part of his oeuvre was published, a rather typical way and moment for a gentleman's works to be brought to the world,
although several other of his writings had to wait considerably
longer before they appeared in print. His *Life of Sidney* was written as a memorial preface to an edition of some of Greville's plays
and verse treatises, but, having come this close to publication, he
stepped back, and the volume never appeared. There may have
been another reason for this in addition to the conventional
motive of aristocratic *hauteur*: since his works had strong
political themes, he may not have wanted to risk his own career at
an especially crucial point when by staying out of print he could
better avoid agitating the Jacobean court gossips.

Greville's philosophic and literary conservatism—his disinclination to react strongly against either the prevailing political
powers or literary modes—should not, however, be emphasized
at the expense of recognizing his intellectual independence. In
both manner and matter his writing reflects a mind dedicated to
wrestling with the intricacies of human existence unremittingly
but also, at times, almost despairingly. The results of this struggle
emerge in a literature that is more compacted with ideas than is
the work of almost any other Renaissance poet. Abraham
Cowley, in the next generation of authors, found him to be "a
vast species apart" from any of his contemporaries.[14] While
Cowley's remark may be thought to be somewhat hyperbolic,
Greville does depart sufficiently from the practices of the poets of
his age so as to make him easily distinguishable, if not always adequately distinguished. C. S. Lewis found him to be a prototypal
existentialist in his skeptical, corrosive attacks on human learning
preparatory to its replacement by divine revelation.[15] The
paradox of ideological writing that leads ultimately to the aboli-
tion of ideology is one that could have been present in several
Renaissance poets but which never fully matured in them in the
way in which it did in Greville. George Gascoigne, for example,
lets pass many of the same sighs of exasperation over human affairs as does Greville, but Gascoigne, to continue the analogy
begun by Lewis, cannot make the existential leap; his poems content themselves with pointing out man's deficiencies without ever
turning to marvel at the awesome grandeur of God. Only Greville
keeps pushing and probing, assaying one attitude and activity
after another, holding on to some longer because they seem to of-

fer some promise of value, before finally abandoning them all as worthless in Jehovah's sight.

Far more radical than the traditional forms in which this examination is carried out is the literary style that Greville came to adopt, a style that must have seemed decidedly unliterary to many of his fellow poets. Shunning the rhetorical flourishes of the English adaptation of the classical *genus grande* or heroic style, largely ignoring the modish Petrarchism mastered so well by Sidney, Greville chose to develop a style that, following Bacon's admonitions for good prose, emphasized content rather than eloquence. Wyatt, especially in his satires, and Gascoigne, among others, had earlier worked in the so-called "plain" style, but Greville used the style with greater flexibility and ingenuity than any of his predecessors. To say this is, of course, to concede partially that he did not always maintain the simplest, plainest literary manner possible, a concession that is a proper one. Greville did start his literary career in the opening poems of *Caelica* as something of a Petrarchist, and, more significantly, even after he had found his own literary voice, he still allowed himself the possibility of adopting a higher style when the form and theme called for it. Thus, as Farmer has observed, in his dramas he uses a middle style so as to accommodate better the speeches of government rulers on public, as well as on private, topics.[16]

It is in his final poems in *Caelica* and in some of his verse treatises that his stylistic achievement becomes most evident. Here, in these dense, somber occasions of genuinely philosophical poetry, he writes in a manner that is more sere and flinty than that of any other major Renaissance poet. Having abandoned love as the *raison d'etre* for his poetry, he abandons as well the adorned language of the lover, a language that he seems to have come increasingly to view as an inaccurate tool for conveying the reality of his world. Unlike Shakespeare, Spenser, or Sidney, he does not elect to celebrate that world's beauty or appeal, only its degeneracy. It is not quite paradoxical, however, to note that the language describing that degeneracy is not without grace, for Greville also avoids the apparently deliberate prosaicness of Gascoigne and Ralegh. His search is for the image of mortal despair that will shatter itself or be shattered as it is replaced by the image of heavenly power. There is, in fact, more art in this style than there is the artlessness that it is sometimes alleged to have, but it is an art that attempts to conceal itself under the import of its theme. Greville was certainly not the only man of his time to believe that man's corrupt nature was the most crucial fact of his existence. But few, if any, other writers were able to order their poetic energies and talents in such a way that the centrality of their belief and the centrality of their art coincided as they do for him.

CHAPTER 2

The Love Poet

GIVEN Greville's pleasure in his intellectual attainments and his friendship with Sidney, it was only reasonable to expect that he would set his hand to the writing of lyric poetry at an early point in his literary career. The example of *Astrophil and Stella* which Sidney was in the process of creating between 1577 and 1580 could not help but inspire Greville to attempt to emulate his friend's achievement. With part of his attention constantly on the fourteenth-century Italian example of Petrarch's series of poems to his mistress Laura, Sidney tried in *Astrophil and Stella* to bring into English some of the grace and imagery of the Italian sonnet cycle, although not necessarily, as David Kalstone has shown, its nearly amoral passion.[1] What neither Sidney nor Greville could have foreseen was the tremendous popularity that the sonnet form was to enjoy during the next twenty years in England, with everyone from the most minor of poets to Shakespeare looking for inspiration to Sidney as a native Petrarch. If Greville began his sonnets in ignorance of the effects that his friend's work would have, he ended them, perhaps twenty-five years later, having seen the full variety of Elizabethan sonnet writing.

Much of that variety is reflected in the one hundred and nine poems that make up the *Caelica* sequence. That not all are son-in the modern sense of the word would not have surprised ⸲⸲zabethan readers, who would have understood the term ⸲ any short poem, but it also true that few poets ⸲he fourteen-line form as thoroughly as did Greville. ⸲one of the poems are sonnets; thirty-five are in six-line ⸲b a b c c); seventeen are in quatrains; the rest furnish ⸲f ottava rima, four-foot trochaics, rhymed sapphics, ⸲ forms indicative of Greville's early disinclination ⸲at some contemporary practice indicated as the limits of a form. Perhaps more surprising is the variety of subjects and characters in the sequence. While most of the sixteenth-century sonnet cycles confined themselves almost exclusively to love and addressed the poems to only one, often-fictive, lady, only about seventy-five poems in *Caelica* are on the subject of love while at least nine are clearly political and eighteen are purely religious in their nature. Of the love poems, the titular heroine Caelica (the heavenly one) is mentioned in twenty-four, while seventeen are directed to Myra, five to Cynthia, and the rest to an unnamed mistress. In fact, however, these nominal fluctuations make very little difference to the progression or lack of it in the sequence, since the women are in no way distinguished from one another. Furthermore, there are virtually no narrative links of any kind between the poems, so the reader necessarily becomes accustomed in all ways to treating the poems as nearly discrete artifacts. Of course, C. S. Lewis' warning of thirty years ago against trying to follow a narrative in the Elizabethan sonnet sequences is still worth remembering,[2] but the fact also remains that at least aspects of a narrative can be glimpsed in most of the other cycles. In Greville's there is virtually none. This is not to say, however, that there is no progression in *Caelica*, for one cannot help but be struck in reading it by the evolution of Greville's interests—an evolution that takes him and the reader from courtly amorous compliment to cynicism about the possibility of any worldly love to rejection of all things of the world for the eternity of God and heaven. The progression advances at varying rates—sometimes abruptly, sometimes eddying—and one can distinguish sections and subsections in the complete sequence. Setting off the first seventy-six poems as the subject of this chapter has the effect of separating out virtually all of the pieces dealing with human love (the remaining sonnets are mainly religious and will be the subject of a following chapter). The changes in attitude that Greville displays toward the experience of love in these seventy-six poems are remarkable in his, or in any, era.

Greville may have wanted at the beginning of *Caelica* to adopt the pose of a true and somewhat awe-struck lover. This, at least, is the stance that he takes in sonnet 1, bringing love, delight, virtue, and reason into conjunction and attributing all of these qualities to his mistress from whose "true heart, cleare springs of wisdome flow, / Which imag'd in her words and deeds, men know."[3] The inherent strength of the opening position is thus

given over to the cycle's most unambiguous praise of the ethic of
the Petrarchan lover and of the woman who is the cause for and
recipient of that love. But even in the following poem, other notes
are being struck as the narrator cries out to the woman in tones
that mix anger and anguish:

> Faire Dog, which so my heart dost teare asunder,
> That my lives-blood, my bowels overfloweth,
> Alas, what wicked rage conceal'st thou under
> These sweet enticing joyes, thy forehead showeth?

In contrast to the at least semiabstract virtues of the first sonnet,
this is a poem of physicality, a description of both the pleasures
and the torments of sexual contemplation without sexual fulfillment. Pleading at the end for her to slay him immediately to
release him from the "fulnesse of the woes, wherein I languish,"
the lover acknowledges the presence of a destructiveness in love
which, if he does not find ultimately to be fatal in the literal
sense, he nevertheless comes to respect sufficiently so as to shun it
as merely one more aspect of general human degradation.

Both Petrarch and Sidney had created narrators who were fond
of bemoaning their plights, but theirs were only intermittent
complaints while Greville's is almost continuous. Even in the
earliest sonnets it is clear that no good can come of the relationship with Caelica; after sonnet 1, everything begins to collapse.
By sonnet 5, Greville is already cursing Cupid for having inspired
some hope in love when a more sensible man could have seen that
women as a species are duplicitous:

> Who by this light God, hath not beene made sory;
> Let him see me eclipsed from my Sunne,
> With shadowes of an Earth quite over-runne.

Of particular interest in this poem is the astronomical setting that
Greville develops in his imagery, with the sun in eclipse corresponding to the afflicted status of the lover. The sense of
physical vastness fraught with peril created by this use of celestial
imagery is, as later discussion will show, one of the most striking
qualities of *Caelica*; Greville returns to the perspective in several
of his very best poems, filling his cosmos alternately with blinding
fire and darkest shade—both images adaptable to either the con-

trasts inherent in the passion of human love or the dichotomy of
fierce divine splendor and worldly corruption.

Sonnet 7 furnishes a good example of the earliest poems in the
sequence:

> The World, that all containes, is ever moving,
> The Starres within their spheres for ever turned,
> Nature (the Queene of Change) to change is loving,
> And Forme to matter new, is still adjourned.
>
> Fortune our phansie-God, to varie liketh,
> Place is not bound to things within it placed,
> The present time upon time passed striketh,
> With Phoebus wandring course the earth is graced.
>
> The Ayre still moves, and by its moving cleareth,
> The Fire up ascends, and planets feedeth,
> The Water passeth on, and all lets weareth,
> The Earth stands still, yet change of changes breedeth;
>
> Her plants, which Summer ripes, in Winter fade,
> Each creature in unconstant mother lyeth,
> Man made of earth, and for whom earth is made,
> Still dying lives, and living ever dyeth;
>   Onely like fate sweet Myra never varies,
>   Yet in her eyes the doome of all Change carries.

The poem opens on an enormous scale ("world," as Bullough
notes, means the universe), emphasizing constant change. Even
the earth, though perforce fixed at the center of the Ptolemaic
cosmos, is depicted as a breeder of cyclical transience. That the
final couplet shows the poem to be "about" a woman is no more
or less surprising than similar "delayed" statements of poetic
thesis in other Renaissance sonnets, but what *is* of importance
here is the manner in which Greville gives and takes back in the
space of two lines. Myra, who in the penultimate line of the poem
is presented as uniquely steadfast, in the final verdict is judged to
be the weathervane of all mutability. As yet, no disaster has
struck, but the connotations surrounding the word "doome" leave
little room for hope.

Greville does take to an extreme this just-mentioned tendency
of his age to remove the woman from the poem. Sometimes, as in

sonnet 7, she appears as subject very late, if at all. In others, such as sonnet 16, she does not even seem to be present as putative audience.

> Fye foolish Earth, thinke you the heaven wants glory,
> Because your shadowes doe your selfe be-night?
> All's darke unto the blind, let them be sory,
> The heavens in themselves are ever bright.
>
> Fye fond desire, thinke you that Love wants glory,
> Because your shadowes doe your selfe benight?
> The hopes and feares of lust, may make men sorie,
> But love still in her selfe finds her delight.
>
> Then Earth stand fast, the skye that you benight
> Will turne againe, and so restore your glory;
> Desire be steady, hope is your delight,
> An orbe wherein no creature can be sorie;
>   Love being plac'd above these middle regions,
>   Where every passion warres it selfe with legions.

In the context of the sequence, one might suggest, as John Shawcross has done, that the poem can be connected with a desire on the lady's part for some manifestation of "glory" in the relationship,[4] but essentially the poem presents the speaker's meditation to himself on the nature of love. Greville again employs cosmic analogues to define genuine love as celestial rather than earthly in nature. The earthbound passions that often think that they are "love" are as darkened and deceived as the side of the earth that is turned away from the sun. If man's baser desires can only learn some measure of patience, the speaker affirms, they will be permitted not only a glimpse of but also participation in the grandeur of higher love.

The extent to which Greville actually believed in such a Platonic ideal of human love is, however, questionable. It is true that the ideal does emerge in the early poems of *Caelica*. Sonnet 10 is one example of this with its claims for love's "glory" and "dazzling brightness." The main business of the poem is, however, to describe the degradation that this ideal undergoes as it passes into the mind of the narrator, a mind ruined by clouded truth, misleading wit, malicious envy, and depressing memory:

> Passion to ruin passion is intended,
> My reason is but power to dissemble;
>   Then tell me Love, what glory you divine
>   Your selfe can find within this soule of mine?

Under the circumstances, he can only advise the spirit of ideal love to go back to the "heavenly quire" of his lady's graces:

> For those sweet glories, which you doe aspire,
> Must, as *Ideas* only be embraced
>   Since excellence in other forme enjoyed,
>   Is by descending to her Saints destroyed.

There is here a simultaneous yearning for the Platonic ideal and a disbelief in the possibility of knowing it in any particularly human manifestation. Richard Waswo, in the most perceptive and detailed analysis yet done of the *Caelica* cycle, says that this poem indicates the presence of a sense of Platonic dualism in Greville that differentiates him from Sidney and the other Neoplatonists. Greville, according to Waswo, "denies the Neoplatonic pretensions to create a continuum, a unity of flesh and spirit in this world. The precise philosophical terms in the poem continue and intensify the irony of adoration: if the descent of excellence from the heaven of Ideas or Forms destroys her, then her saints are spurious and their worship far from divine."[5] In several poems in *Astrophil and Stella* (see, especially, sonnets 5, 21, and 25) Sidney shows not only a clear awareness of the combination of virtue, reason, and passion posited by Plato in the *Phaedrus* as the basis for genuine love but also a recognition that this is the course that his narrator as a lover ought to take. Greville, however, rarely, if ever, sees any point in referring his amorous feelings to the supposedly governing force of virtuous reason. The discontinuity between the ideal of love and what his speaker has found to be its actual practice is so great that there is no particular point in trying to dignify his passion for his mistress on rational grounds.

The prevalent attitude toward the amorous experience in the first half of *Caelica* is thus one that stresses this worldly actuality of human passion, for both the better and the worse. As should be apparent by now, Greville's opinion of love is frequently negative, more negative than in any other Elizabethan sonnet sequence. In sonnet 21, for example, the speaker accuses the doubleness of women:

Sathan, no Woman, yet a wandring spirit,
When he saw ships saile two wayes with one wind,
Of Saylers trade he hell did disinherit:
The Divell himselfe loves not a halfe-fast mind.

The Satyre when he saw the Shepheard blow
To warme his hands, and make his pottage coole,
Manhood forsweares, and halfe a beast did know,
Nature with double breath is put to schoole.

Cupid doth head his shafts in Womens faces,
Where smiles and teares dwell ever neere together,
Where all the Arts of Change give Passion graces;
While these clouds threaten, who feares not the weather?
    Saylers and Satyres, Cupids Knights, and I
    Feare Women that Sweare, Nay; and know they lye.

Carrying the argument by means of analogies to ships able to sail
in two directions in the same wind and a shepherd's using his
breath both to warm and to cool, Greville attacks what he takes
to be the feminine tendency to encourage and banish a lover nearly simultaneously.

But if the general point of this sonnet is clear, one must also
concede that Greville does not seem concerned with removing all
obscurity from it. The third line of each of the two opening
quatrains complicates both the sense and the syntax of the statement. The proverblike formulations of lines four and eight are
clear enough, and the stories told in each of the quatrains may
perhaps not have been unknown to an educated Elizabethan, but
that hardly explains, in the case of the first quatrain, why Satan
should choose to make it impossible for hell to possess "Saylers
trade" or, indeed, what is meant by "trade" and how Satan got
control of it in the first place.

The difficulty is not limited to this particular poem, but is present throughout *Caelica* more often than one would like. At some
points it is limited to an obscure phrase, to a locution that is
nonidiomatic and rather contorted. But at other moments the
obscurity expands to encompass a sentence or perhaps an entire
stanza. The more frequently these obscurities occur, the more difficult it becomes to avoid concluding that Greville's talent was
sometimes simply insufficient for the task of consistently rendering reasonably complex ideas into metered speech. He can display

a tendency toward what might be called a kind of poetic con-
stipation: he often seems to be laboring too hard to express
himself, with a resultant loss of clarity. Or, to place a more
charitable construction on the matter, perhaps the style can be
seen as an artistic corollary of a mind too doubtful and tentative
to commit itself clearly to one explicit position. In any case, his
obscurity is rarely exasperating, since one almost always must
acknowledge the poetic force of his images and concepts, even
those that are imprecisely stated. Greville risks more thematically
than most of his contemporaries, and it should therefore be no
surprise if he has occasional lapses in execution.

As one continues to read through the poems in *Caelica*, one is
struck by the increasing originality of the lyrics. If the standard
view that the numbering of the sonnets is indicative of their order
of composition is correct, Greville clearly became a more confident poet as he went along. Few modern readers will find many
of the first forty poems in the cycle to be particularly memorable.
In them, Greville is by and large content with the conventional
subjects of the love lyric as he found them articulated by Sidney,
Dyer, and their English and continental predecessors. The
number of "genuine" (i.e., fourteen-line) sonnets is significantly
greater here, and Greville rarely moves beyond the traditional
complaints to his mistress or to Cupid. He clearly knows how to
use the conventions, and, as has been suggested, he probably
believed in the conventional stance of suffering to a greater extent
than one would expect to be the case with a Renaissance sonneteer, but only rarely does he strike upon the happy coincidence
of a new idea and forceful expression. One cannot help but be
pleased, therefore, to find a poem such as sonnet 39 with its surprising analogue between the Tower of Babel and the lover's relationship with Caelica.

> The pride of Flesh by reach of humane wit,
> Did purpose once to over-reach the skye;
> And where before God drown'd the world for it,
> Yet Babylon it built up, not to dye.
>
> God knew these fooles how foolishly they wrought,
> That Destiny with Policie would breake,
> Straight none could tell his fellow what he thought,
> Their tongues were chang'd, & men not taught to speake:

So I that heavenly peace would comprehend,
In mortall seat of Caelica's faire heart,
To babylon my selfe there, did intend,
With naturall kindnesse, and with passions art:
    But when I thought my selfe of her selfe free,
    All's chang'd: She understands all men but me.

Hoping to strengthen his position in Caelica's estimation ("to babylon myself" in her heart) by manifesting an intense (though perhaps overly studied) love, he suffers the same irony of mutual unintelligibility that afflicted the ambitious builders in Genesis; she shows no acknowledgment of what he has done. The shock of seeing the biblical story put to this use is an intriguing one. Greville has found his own poetic voice.

The following poem, sonnet 40, is remarkable among other reasons for the ways in which it anticipates the *carpe diem* motif of the early seventeenth century. Caelica and Caelica's influence over the poet are compared to organic growth, eventually to the development of a rose, but first and most importantly to the beauty of ripening grain, the "nurse-life Wheat." The classical *carpe diem* poets and their seventeenth-century heirs stress the brevity of a plant's flourishing in order to enforce more vigorously the importance of loving without delay. Greville initially seems to draw a different conclusion from his study of the process, stating that "faire and sweet is the bud, more sweet and faire / The Rose, which proves that time is not destroying." But by the end of the poem with its return to the notion of the cyclical ripening of the wheat, he shows a clear awareness of the fact that Caelica's mature beauty (her "ripe yeeres love-noone") has attained a peak (it will go "no higher"). What matters ultimately for him, though, is neither time past nor time yet to come but the intensity of feeling at the present moment. The warmth of this amorous noon vaporizes all of his life spirits into "desire," a desire that is clearly physical rather than spiritual.

In the poems that follow, there is an ever more direct recognition of the force of this desire and a concomitant effort to denigrate any remnant of idealism in the love relationship. A strong note of cynicism enters the poems as the speaker sets about analyzing the weakness and degeneracy manifested by his addiction to love while simultaneously acknowledging that he enjoys at least some aspects of his situation. In sonnet 41 he laughs scornfully at his "poore soule" for persisting to think that "constant faith" and "true devotion" will win favor from his mistress (Myra, this time), since it has become clear to him intellectually that she has been unfaithful to him and will be so again with no regard for his feelings. Still addressing his soul and still scoffing at the soul for its optimism, he ends the poem in a rebuke to his spirit for

> Hoping to make that constant, which is ill;
> Therefore the doome is, wherein thou must rest,
> Myra that scornes thee, shall love many best.

This indictment of woman's fidelity has its echoes throughout the cycle. The speaker is never emotionally devastated by the idea of unfaithfulness; indeed, he is quite calm and accepting, acknowledging that love is shattered permanently by woman's deceit but never hoping for anything better. Rebholz has recently noted that about half of the first seventy-seven poems in *Caelica* have infidelity as a principal theme,[6] a proportion so high that it becomes extremely difficult to call these lyrics "love" poems in any normal sense of the word. The explanation for this frequency is to be found, Rebholz believes, in Greville's profound convictions on the corruption of human nature after the fall.[7] Female infidelity, in this view, becomes one easily noted manifestation of postlapsarian human nature and is thus the most logical subject to be singled out for special attention in a series of poems on the relationship between the sexes.

This deterioration of human status is sometimes presented directly as the thesis of a poem. Sonnet 44, for example, contrasts love in the present age with what it had been in the mythical Edenic Golden Age of precivilized and presophisticated society. The speaker makes the not-uncommon Renaissance equation of his own era with the Age of Brass: "now when Earth is worne, / Beauty growne sicke, Nature corrupt and nought, / Pleasure untimely dead as soone as borne." In this brazen epoch "The old Lord knowes Desire is poorely fed, / And sorrowes not a wavering province lost." Women are going to be false, but whether a specific betrayal is a product of a changed environment or rather contributes to that environment's decline it is hard to say, so thoroughly interrelated are the mores of individuals and their era.

What prevents this ascetic, *contemptu mundi* attitude from

prevailing completely and turning *Caelica* away from its original subject at this point is the speaker's continuing fascination with what women and sexual desire do to him. In sonnet 45 Greville takes up a subject that had been the inspiration for Sidney several times in *Astrophil and Stella*—the lovers' separation—but treats it in a way very different from Sidney. Giving the topic at least two ironic twists, Greville's speaker, unlike Sidney's, at first professes to be grateful for absence, since he feels, among other things, that it makes him love more intensely:

> Absence doth nurse the fire,
> Which starves and feeds desire
> With sweet delayes.

But this apparent detachment cannot be maintained forever, and the poem closes with a sudden reverse:

> But Thoughts be not so brave,
> With absent joy;
> For you with that you have
> Your selfe destroy:
> The absence which you glory,
> Is that which makes you sory,
> And burne in vaine:
> For Thought is not the weapon,
> Wherewith thoughts-ease men cheapen,
> Absence is paine.

It has been the function of the two-foot line to oppose or qualify the three-foot line throughout the poem, but this final two-foot line, as Thom Gunn observes, is even more distinct from what has gone before than usual.[8] The light, witty irony of praise of absence is replaced by a more somber irony expressive of the mind's inability to compensate for the anguish of passionate desire that goes unfulfilled.

While Greville chooses most frequently to develop his ideas on love in the meditative form of the short lyric, there are occasional poems where narration predominates. Sonnet 56, deservedly one of the better-known poems in the sequence, is such an instance. The story of the 55-line poem (79-line in the manuscript version) begins at night with the speaker aroused to go out in search of his mistress:

> All my senses, like Beacons flame,
> Gave Alarum to desire
> To take armes in Cynthia's name,
> And set my thoughts on fire.

The error of the speaker's ways turns out to be excessive emphasis on the "thoughts" generated by the appeal to his "senses." Intellectualizing and idealizing the situation excessively while on his nocturnal stroll, he feels as though he is being "borne up to the skyes" by Cynthia's heavenly beauty. Even granted the fact that his mistress' name is that of the goddess of the moon, the narrator can arouse nothing but suspicion in the reader as he proceeds to soar beyond reality: "I stept forth to touch the skye, / I a God by Cupid dreames." The upshot is that he loses Cynthia, who had apparently been ready and waiting for less celestial experiences:

> Cynthia who did naked lye,
> Runnes away like silver streames;
> Leaving hollow banks behind.

Left with nothing, the narrator can only moralize, as he says, like a man about to be executed. No one, he maintains, should wait once he has his mistress "naked on a bed of play." Any procrastination or gazing into the stars at that point is, he now ruefully acknowledges, wasted time: "None can well behold with eyes, / But what underneath him lies." To think and act otherwise is to be hopelessly idealistic; love of the flesh can be consummated, but mythologized, Petrarchan love of the soul can only delude. It is an antiromantic point that has been made before in an implicit way in the cycle, but the directness of the statement here has an engaging quality that distinguishes the poem from most of the others.

Since the first seventy-six poems in *Caelica* were presumably written at intervals between 1577 and 1587, a decade as busy as any in Greville's life, it would be an unrealistic reader indeed who would expect the cycle to display an even and sustained level of poetic accomplishment. Every now and then, however, a cluster of poems coheres as a successful unit. One such group is the four-poem sequence that begins with sonnet 61 and ends with sonnet 64. The themes taken up in this set are in the main familiar by this point in *Caelica*—recognition of the irrational power of love set off against a cynical self-abasement for having played the

role of lover—but they are developed with verve and wit in
larger-than-customary quantities.

   In sonnet 61 Greville's speaker contemplates the deterioration
of his affair with Caelica with a sense of cool detachment and,
this time, an admission of his own infidelity. Whenever she
swears that she prefers him to all other men he feels trapped by
her, helpless as a baby strapped into a cradle who can only smile
at his nurse and gesticulate his desires for liberty. At moments like
this, painfully aware of his own "broken vowes," he is at a loss as
to which of two childish impulses to follow—continued wrong-
doing or sheepish apology. In these periods of uncertainty he has
come to believe that constancy is only a fiction and love only
genuine to the extent that the moment allows it to be:

> Love is no true made Looking-glasse,
> Which perfect yeelds the shape we bring,
> It ugly showes us all that was,
> And flatters every future thing.
>   When Phoebus beames no more appeare,
>   Tis darker that the day was here.

Although calling Change a "hatefull power," he nevertheless
acknowledges that he and Caelica have both been subject to it. In
such instances of mutually *un*reciprocated "love" it is clear to him
that "constant faith is made a drudge." As a consequence of their
tangled relationship, the speaker now ends by simultaneously
congratulating himself that he is no self-pitying fool, bidding her
good-riddance, feeling guilt for his own actions, and suffering
pain from her cruelty to him. In its exploration of impassioned
and often contradictory feelings the poem anticipates much of
what Donne was to do a few years later.

   Again like Donne, Greville's seemingly instinctive proclivity is
to evaluate earthly events and emotions in comparison to supernature and eternity. The fact that the comparison is made at all is
indicative of the conclusions and priorities that both poets
ultimately achieve and maintain. While earlier sonnets in *Caelica*
have been located in a celestial setting, not until sonnet 62 does
Greville show a clear awareness of a conflict between love and
religion. The first three stanzas take up focal points of man's interest—love, war, and politics, respectively, presenting each in
terms of the planets that exert astrological influence over these activities. The fourth and final stanza then proceeds to dismiss these

planetary gods as earthly, in fact, rather than heavenly, and
urges the reader to set his sights beyond them.

> Mercurie, Cupid, Mars, they be no Gods,
> But humane Idols, built up by desire,
> Fruit of our boughs, whence heaven maketh rods,
> And babyes too for child-thoughts that aspire:
>> Who sees their glories, on the earth must prye;
>> Who seeks true glory must looke to the skye.

With this, the "true glory" of religion has taken its place at the
head of Greville's scale of values, a position that it was to maintain for the rest of his career.

Against religion's glory and wisdom, Greville sets man's im-
potence and blindness. This contrast, so frequently present in his
later writing, is also developed in these middle poems in *Caelica*.
Sonnet 63 opens with the evaluative claim that "the greatest pride
of humane kind is Wit" and then proceeds to list examples of
man's vain attempts to reason about a variety of natural phe-
nomena. Just as the divine "Infinite" and powerful "Chance" are
"farre exceeding" of the limits of reason, so is love, for "no wit can
comprehend the wayes of Love." Whatever slim possibility man
might have of understanding his circumstances when he is in love
is denied by the nature and force of the passion itself. Although
qualitatively far different from divinity and the power of chance,
its effects can be equally unamenable to rational interpretation.
The speaker thus concludes with the traditional (but here fully
earned) acknowledgment that "they once had eyes, that are made
blind by love."

Sonnet 64 turns religious diction to satirical ends in contrasting
the narrator's perceptions of Caelica before and after their falling
out of love. The first two quatrains of this Shakespearian-style
sonnet present her in her earlier Petrarchan incarnation of
heavenly ideal, someone so virtuous as to be superior to any
"earthly metall." But in the witty sestet spiritual elegance is replaced by mortal womanly fickleness. "Since my fall" from her
grace, the speaker has lost the quondam divine vision. Now he
sees only "your backe, while all the world beholds your face."
This accusation of infidelity brings sarcasm into the poem as he
professes still to find "miracles" in the glimpses that he catches of
her. Her heart, he sneers, still must be "a heavenly place":

> For what before was fill'd by me alone,
> I now discerne hath roome for every one.

Greville expands his analysis of unfaithfulness in sonnet 67, equating duplicity of character and betrayal in love. Both traits are, in his analysis, manifestations of the same moral corruption, a corruption that, by this point in the sequence, he attributes to both sexes:

> Unconstant thoughts where light desires do move,
> With every object which sense to them showes,
> Still ebbing from themselves to Seas of Love,
> Like ill led Kings that conquer but to lose,
>> With blood and paine these dearely purchase shame,
>> Time blotting all things out, but evill name.
>
> The double heart that loveth it selfe best,
> Yet can make selfe-love beare the name of friend,
> Whose kindnesse onely in his wit doth rest,
> And can be all but truth, to have his end,
>> Must one desire in many figures cast;
>> Dissemblings then are knowne when they are past.
>
> The heart of man mis-seeking for the best,
> Oft doubly or unconstantly must blot,
> Betweene these two the misconceipt doth rest,
> Whether it ever were that lasteth not,
>> Unconstancy and doublenesse depart,
>> When man bends his desires to mend his heart.

Each of the first two stanzas takes one of the two deficiencies as its subject, showing its causes and its effects, and leaving it to the third stanza to draw the two together with its sententious pointing out of the essential similarities. Rebholz feels that the poem's controlled rhythm and its use of vividly concrete verbs and metaphors as a balance to the abstraction of its topics makes it a good example of Greville's mature style.[9] The impression made by the poem is certainly one of judicious wisdom conveyed in the tone of a man who has long observed human frailty, who has no particular hope of its amelioration, but who is not so weathered and cynical that he feels it pointless to comment on the subject. This is exactly the kind of speaker who is most comfortable with generalization and abstraction, but it must be noted that Greville's generalizations do not drift, that they almost invariably come to a conclusive point. Waswo has observed how often Greville relies on the terseness of aphorisms as a means of enforcing the moral of an abstraction for the reader.[10] Each of the three stanzas in sonnet 67 concludes with an aphorism, only the first of which was commonly known and, therefore, proverbial. In the other cases here, and elsewhere in his writing, Greville shows the Renaissance trait of creating and using aphorism as a means of logical proof rather than as merely substantiating ornament. His sententiae, and these are fair examples, are usually apposite and succinct in form and almost always mordant and pejorative in matter.

The cynicism about love that has been building as the cycle has developed culminates in the magnificent despair of sonnet 69. The perspective of the opening stanza of this poem is unmatched anywhere in Greville's work. It would doubtless be impossible for any poet to sustain this initial grandeur, and the poem declines markedly in the two remaining stanzas:

> When all this All doth passe from age to age,
> And revolution in a circle turne,
> Then heavenly Justice doth appeare like rage,
> The Caves doe roare, the very Seas doe burne,
>   Glory growes darke, the Sunne becomes a night,
>   And makes this great world feele a greater might.
>
> When Love doth change his seat from heart to heart,
> And worth about the wheele of Fortune goes,
> Grace is deseas'd, desert seemes overthwart,
> Vowes are forlorne, and truth doth credit lose,
>   Chance then gives Law, Desire must be wise,
>   And looke more wayes than one, or lose her eyes.
>
> My age of joy is past, of woe begunne,
> Absence my presence is, strangenesse my grace,
> With them that walke against me, is my Sunne:
> The wheele is turn'd, I hold the lowest place,
>   What can be good to me since my love is,
>   To doe me harme, content to doe amisse?

With overtones of the Judgment Day, the first stanza describes the changing of the Great Year, a concept from classical astronomy that emphasizes the transformations of enormous magnitude that supposedly occur at regular intervals in the history of the universe. Analogically dwarfed in comparison, changes in love come to seem not only inevitable but also relatively inconsequential. Fidelity and truth in love go unrewarded, but love operates, after all, in a world that now seems controlled by nonhuman forces. If he is spurned by his mistress the lover is also at the bottom of larger wheels of fortune. The nature of the cyclical imagery that controls the poem implies a sort of eventual justice, however remote that possibility might seem at the moment. The poet's only hope apparently resides in the distant reaches of this divine scheme.

After sonnet 69 the remaining six poems belonging to the amorous series in *Caelica* invariably strike the reader as a falling-off. Lacking any substantial continuity, either among themselves or with the poems preceding them, they seem to reflect an uncertainty on Greville's part as to where to turn next in his poetry. It seems distinctly possible that they may be efforts that had been worked out at various times in Greville's career and that he chose to include them in the manuscript at this point for the sake of completeness. Of these poems, sonnet 71 comes closest to continuing the themes of disillusionment about love that he had been developing in the cycle. Cupid speaks in the poem to defend himself against charges of malfeasance of duty. Acknowledging his defeat and contrasting his fall from his paradise as a lover with that of Adam from Eden, the god vows that he will "follow Women-kinde" no longer, choosing instead to aim for the ideals of "Knowledge, Honour, Fame, or Honestie," a virtual program of the subjects of Greville's subsequent poetry: "And I no more will stirre this earthly dust, / Wherein I lose my name, to take on lust."

Sonnets 74 and 75 are long (62 and 228 lines, respectively), rambling narrative poems that neither engage the interest nor seem typical of Greville. They represent older, more conventional attitudes toward pastoral love, and they attempt to develop their motifs in a similar, but far less successful, manner to that of Sidney in the songs that are interspersed in *Astrophil and Stella*.

The odd mixtures of subjects and tones in these final poems confirm what would have been clear enough had Greville stopped with sonnet 69: that he had reached a dead end in the development of his ideas on earthly love. Having negated any worth that might once have been attached to emotion between the sexes, Greville was clearly prepared now to look elsewhere in his search for ultimate value.

CHAPTER 3

The Dramatist

G REVILLE wrote three plays: *Alaham, Antony and Cleopatra,* and *Mustapha.* Only *Alaham* and *Mustapha* are extant, the latter in three different versions. Rebholz argues for the existence at one point of four different manuscript versions of *Alaham,* but since we have today only the text of the 1633 posthumous edition of Greville's plays, the others cannot be of major concern to us.[1] *Mustapha,* in addition to the 1633 test, also exists in a printed text of 1609 (an edition obviously done without Greville's permission) and in two essentially identical manuscripts both of which probably precede the 1609 edition.[2] Some aspects of these earlier versions of the play are of interest for their capacity to demonstrate the evolution of Greville's thought and dramatic skill. In the main, however, the 1633 version of the play, the one that represents Greville's final intentions, is the version that most justifiably merits analysis, and it is that version that we shall examine.[3]

Greville's interest in writing drama was probably spurred by Mary Sidney, countess of Pembroke, in the mid-1590s, and this period presumably contains the date of the first version of *Mustapha. Alaham* and *Antony and Cleopatra* come somewhat later, at about the turn of the century, certainly before the abortive rebellion of the earl of Essex in February 1601. It was this event, in fact, that caused Greville to destroy the manuscript of *Antony and Cleopatra.* He apparently felt that it was politically imprudent to preserve a play that presented a man's reckless passion for a female monarch, or so he suggested some years later in an autobiographical passage in the *Life of Sidney:* "many members in that creature [*Antony and Cleopatra*] (by the opinion of those few eyes, which saw it) having some childish wantonnesse in them, apt enough to be construed, or strained to a personating of vices in the present Governors, and government."[4]

That he never returned to the dramatic form except to revise *Mustapha* is perhaps indicative of a preference that he developed for other literary genres as conveyors of sentiments and opinions that were increasingly personal.

I   *Greville and the Senecan Drama*

Alaham and *Mustapha* invariably strike the reader as difficult, rather obscure plays when compared with other contemporary drama. Some of this difficulty derives from the complexity and the emotional uneasiness of the plays' ideology, while still more is attributable to our age's lack of sympathy for the Senecan tradition in which Greville is working.

The influences of the Latin tragedian Seneca on the literature of the English Renaissance are diverse and complicated. In what was predominately a Latin intellectual culture, it was only natural that Rome's most significant writer of tragedy should be taken as a model by at least some native English dramatists. The model may not have been the best, since modern criticism has been rather severe with Seneca for his imperfect continuation of the traditions of Greek drama and for his tendency to give his plays over to long declamatory speeches. Nevertheless, to the English lover of drama in the sixteenth century, Seneca was the logical author to look to for inspiration in the development of modern tragedy. Seneca had already had homage done to him by moderns in Italy and France, and, indeed, the imitation of "Seneca" that goes on in England in the sixteenth century is frequently an imitation of his later continental followers.

As English tragedy came into existence in the second half of the sixteenth century, it unfailingly depended on Seneca for its tone and content. These early examples of English tragedies were almost exclusively created by academicians for academic audiences, so the indebtedness to sources would be both apparent and admired. Thomas Norton and Thomas Sackville's *Gorboduc* (1561), to name the earliest example, has a balanced, five-act Senecan structure, each act closing with a chorus that sums up and comments on the action. This action often takes the form of violent revenge, an idea that Seneca held to be central to the concept of tragedy, but dramatic decorum required that much of this violence be reported by a nuntius (messenger). His speeches, like those of the rest of the characters, are long, didactic, and highly rhetorical.

As long as tragedy stayed in academic milieux the adherence to Senecan principles was fairly rigorous. But when with Thomas Kyd's *The Spanish Tragedy* (1586) the popular theater took on several of the Senecan techniques the resulting hybrid showed an intriguing flexibility that a rote following of the Senecan "rules" could not afford. It was, in fact, this union of the classical and the popular stages that was to produce some of the finest Elizabethan tragedies, including Marlowe's *Tamburlaine* in 1587 and Shakespeare's *Richard III*, perhaps his most Senecan play, in 1592.

Greville's interest in the Senecan form does not, however, derive from this acceptance of the Roman author by the popular playwrights. It seems likely that it was his presence in the literary circle centering on the countess of Pembroke that drew him originally to the drama. The countess's translation in 1592 of *Marc Antoine*, a play by the French Senecan Robert Garnier, seems to have set off yet another revival of interest in Seneca.[5] In the decade that followed, Samuel Daniel, Thomas Kyd, Samuel Brandon, and William Alexander all joined Greville and the countess in writing or translating from French a group of plays treating in the Senecan manner events and characters from Roman history. Geoffrey Bullough has observed that one of the common denominators of these plays (though we can, of course, only suppose about Greville's destroyed Roman play) is their treatment of their historical material in a way that emphasizes political example rather than dramatic conflict between individuals.[6]

These plays were all intended for the study rather than the stage. Kyd was the only member of the group with any interest in the popular theater, but he surely wanted to try to establish his social credentials with his Roman play and made it conform to the nondramatic mode of his social betters. The modern reader should not be too hasty in dismissing these plays as devoid of interest when compared to the popular Elizabethan drama. One must simply read them with a different set of demands than one would bring to a play of Shakespeare. Intended to challenge the intellect with the exposition of serious political and moral problems, these plays need to be judged as works of philosophy cast into the external form of the drama.

Furthermore, one needs to think carefully about the sense in which these works are *not* designed for the stage. Greville's own pronouncement on the subject in the *Life of Sidney* would seem to be ambiguous: "I have made these Tragedies, no Plaies for the Stage. . . . But he that will behold these Acts upon their true Stage, let him look on that Stage wherein himself is an Actor, even the state he lives in, and for every part he may perchance find a Player, and for every Line (it may be) an instance of life."[7] What needs to be noticed here is the distinction that Greville seems to be making between staged plays and the drama as a literary form. The former is merely entertainment and therefore an appropriate recipient of the attacks that the Puritans were waging against it throughout the period, while the latter engages the mind seriously and leads to important discoveries about the nature of life. The distinction may not, however, be as sharp as Greville would like to think it to be, since for most readers of drama the form inevitably leads to mental staging. Greville's social and moral motives for shunning the popular theater are in no sense, then, motives that would make it impossible for him to *imagine* his plays' being staged any more than it was difficult for Milton to envision the staging of *Samson Agonistes*. That the plays are not particularly dramatic and that it is questionable if an audience could be found willing to sit through a performance are not comments on artistic genre but rather on Greville's deficiencies as a creative artist.

These deficiencies need to be admitted in order that Greville's dramatic achievement might be kept in a proper perspective. *Mustapha* and *Alaham* are extraordinarily stiff and in some ways confusing plays. Some of these difficulties are attributable to the Senecan conventions—the use of a nuntius or a chorus can stop a play dead—but the stiffness extends beyond what the following of convention can excuse. In some scenes drama becomes almost totally impossible when a character seemingly ignores whoever else might be listening to soliloquize interminably. But Greville, we must remember, had had little contact with the realities of staging.

II   *Subjects and Sources*

Among his fellow Elizabethan Senecans, Greville is unique in his choice of modern plots for his plays. If, however, they deal with events contemporaneous to Greville, it should also be said that their Oriental settings do serve to distance them from the reader to at least the extent that would a plot from classical Roman history. With *Mustapha* located in Turkey and *Alaham* in the Arab kingdom of Ormus, the plays possess an exoticism that causes the reader to evaluate their characters and plots in a rather different way than would be the case with a more familiar setting.

Oriental stories, though not commonplace, were by no means unprecedented as sources for Elizabethan literature. Interest in exploration and in exotica in general had insured that no small number of narratives, both fictive and historical, had found their way into print in England and in other Western European countries. Bullough has studied the possible sources for Greville's dramas and has explained in considerable detail both Greville's fidelity to extant tales and his divergences from them.[8] The *Alaham* story seems to have its principal source in an Italian travel narrative, the *Itinerary* of Ludovico di Varthema, first published in Rome in 1510. Varthema's story tells of the murder of a doddering sultan of Ormus by his ambitious son. A revolt by the masses ensues, and no peace is to be found until a slave of the old Sultan kills the usurping son and goes on to act as regent for the usurper's younger brother. The basic elements of *Alaham*'s plot are here, though Greville also departs drastically from his source in his conception of the old Sultan's slave whom he names Mahomet and elevates to the function of basha or counselor. The reasons for the change are important to an understanding of Greville's interest in the story and will be taken up shortly.

The question of the source for *Mustapha* is more complicated since the story of the Turkish sultan Soliman the Magnificent was more widely known. Generally feared throughout Europe in the sixteenth century, Soliman had become the subject of numerous histories and commentaries as well as of two dramas written prior to Greville's. The title of the play names Soliman's son who was known to have been an innocent victim of his father's fears of rebellion, fears that had been fed by Soliman's wife, Mustapha's stepmother, who hoped to place her own son, Mustapha's younger half-brother, in the line of succession. Some, though by no means all, of the sources tell of Achmat, a counselor of the monarch, who recognizes the errors of the sultan's ways but who remains loyal to him to preserve the stability of the state. That

Greville draws upon those sources that mention Achmat in composing his eclectic version of the story is indicative of his abiding
interest in the role of the uncertain counselor. The role is one that
Greville undoubtedly saw as having autobiographical implications and one with which he was free to be both severe in his self-
criticism and charitable in his presentation of a man in a difficult
situation.

Although one might at first suppose that such parallels would
not readily offer themselves in plays with Oriental settings,
Greville in fact is able to develop virtually whatever analogue he
might want for his contemporary situation. Although the action
of the plays takes place in nominally non-Christian countries,
Greville the Christian moralist presents his characters with
political and personal dilemmas to which they are forced to respond in terms of Christian values. Joan Rees, in her comparison
of the early and the revised versions of *Mustapha*, has shown that
one of the principal effects of Greville's revision of the play was to
heighten the sense of Christian conflict in the drama, to emphasize, for example, the otherworldliness of the innocent son
Mustapha and the materialism of all those who surround him.[9]
The theme was present in the earlier version, but its more forceful
restatement in the revision is indicative of what must have been a
growing desire on Greville's part to accentuate what had come to
him to be a vital issue.

A connected theme, one present in both plays, is the nature of
the relationship between the state and the church which Greville
saw as constantly in danger of being seduced and destroyed morally by becoming as worldly as the society whose souls it pur-
portedly protected. Or, to come at the same issue from the
perspective of the state, to what extent, Greville asks, can a temporal leader remain pure and take on some of the virtues of the
cleric while at the same time performing his necessary duties?
This largely explains his interest in both plays in the role of the
counselor to the monarch, the man who must attempt to preserve
the fabric of a stable social order while simultaneously answering
to God for what he knows to be the wrongs that he is forced to
commit in doing so. Since, in Greville's system of thought, such
"wrongs" are inevitably conceptualized as sin, a breaking of
God's will, there is yet another, still larger, theme brought into
the drama—an examination of the nature of sin. All political ac-

tion leads to personal sin, but to refrain from politics for that reason is to commit yet another sin, that of cowardice in leadership. It is in this problematic situation that Greville places his most sympathetic characters, knowing that they have no way out but knowing too that to ignore their dilemma would be to fail to confront the situation that he had personally found to be the most vexing one of his life.

III   Alaham

Although *Alaham* was probably composed after the early version of *Mustapha*, I choose to discuss it first because it manifests certain practices in organization, theme, and style that Greville was to bring to a higher state of perfection in the final version of *Mustapha*. Professor Bullough dates *Alaham* at about 1600, partly because he thinks that the character sketches in the play's prologue may have been influenced by Ben Jonson's similar device in *Every Man out of His Humour*, a play written in 1599.[10]

Greville probably had read Varthema's narrative of the sultan of Ormus in the original Italian edition, though the work had been translated into virtually all of the Western European languages by the end of the sixteenth century. What Greville and other interested readers had found in Varthema's story of the ambitious and usurping son was that favored Elizabethan motif of the overreacher. The author who best developed the theme was Marlowe, and, in spite of the very different traditions in which the playwrights are working, there are some clear affinities between the titular protagonists of *Alaham* and *Tamburlaine* (1587; printed, 1590). Like Marlowe's conqueror, Alaham is frequently seized by fits of bombast, apparently believing that his capacity to impose his will on others is directly connected to his capacity to describe his desires in the most hyperbolic of ranting:

> And am I King? And doe my foes still live?
> Can wounded Greatnesse slumber in a Throne?
> Or that be glory which I feele alone?
> No, No: Let rigour speake, which all men heare:
> Life, is the worke of Nature; death, of Kings:
> Ruine it is, that reputation brings.
>
> (III, i, 21–26)[11]

In the character of Alaham we are given what is potentially
one of the most stirring of dramatic spectacles: a man who, like
Milton's Satan, deliberately chooses evil as his good and who is
willing to deal with whatever consequences his choice might
bring. Greville's shortcoming, however, in the rendering of that
character is a failure to specify in sufficient detail the evolu-
tionary stages of Alaham's grand passions. It is a problem that,
Una Ellis-Fermor thinks, he shares with Marlowe: a tendency to
present abstractions in a manner that leaves the ideology relatively independent of the stimulus of character or personality.[12] The
play as a whole can become rather frustrating for the reader
because of this bifurcation of theme and character. There is, to be
sure, something very simple about the plot and its story of ambition undone, but there is also an excess of complexity, of unex-
plained motives and actions in the development of that plot.

In a prologue spoken by a ghost of a former king of Ormus, the
reader is given succinct sketches of each of the characters. This
laying-out of dominant traits as well as of the outcome for each
character naturally removes the possibility of suspense from the
overall effect of the play, although no Renaissance tragedian ever
placed a very high priority on that particular quality. Indeed, in
the opening scene of the play, a conversation between Alaham
and the priest Heli, Alaham divulges much of his plan at once. He
wants the throne badly and sees the killing of his older brother as
the first step along what he understands will be a bloody path to
the achieving of that goal. When Heli tries to dissuade him and
counsels patience, Alaham cuffs him aside with a brusque "Who
measures hopes, and losses by the truth, / Goes ever naked in this
world of might" (I, i, 199–200). Heli objects again upon learning
that part of Alaham's scheme involves using the church to consoli-
date his power. If, he warns Alaham with virtuous indignation,

> . . . you . . . make the Church your stayres,
> By which you clime your owne ambitious way;
> Your glory will be short, and full of feares.
> (I, i, 228–30)

Alaham, however, sees the church as only one more tool of policy:
"The Church it is one linke of Government, / Of noblest Kings
the noblest instrument" (I, i, 237–38). Heli's opposition collapses
in front of this cool cynicism about the political malleability of

the church, and Alaham has his way. He closes the scene on stage
alone, invoking the evil spirits of "blacke eternity" to help him in
his task of bringing "ruine, and change." The scene is an effective
opening to the play in that it brings us directly into the tormented
mind of Alaham and shows us his tendency to move almost immediately back and forth from the most practical matters of external affairs to the intensely personal "visions . . . of better
hopes, . . . malice, and rage" (I, i, 185–86). Furthermore, in introducing the important theme of the political manipulation of
the church at this early point, Greville spotlights it and asks that
the reader give it his immediate attention.

The only other character in the play who initiates action is
Hala, Alaham's wife, introduced in a soliloquy at the beginning
of the second act. Although she despises her husband, she is
similar to him in her energy and her capacity to leap from introspective sessions of hate-distilling to active strategies of conniving. Lustful and ambitious, she pretends to embrace her husband's strategems while actually wanting to advance to power
herself in the company of her lover Caine, a royal counselor. In
the opening three scenes of act 2, Greville shows her successively
alone, with Alaham, and with Caine. As one scene follows upon
another, we see the working out of the maxim with which she had
closed her opening soliloquy: "Who hides his minde is to himselfe
a friend." Candid with no one but herself, she first claims to want
to help Alaham in his plan to kill both Caine and Mahomet,
another counselor, whom he sees as the two men most immediately cutting him off from the throne. When she is with Caine she
again camouflages her real nature behind the rhetoric with which
she turns a basically weak, indecisive man (she doubtless could
not live with a strong one) to her purpose of killing Alaham and
Mahomet. Her power over Caine is such that he immediately
gives up all sense of self: "It is not I that live in me, but
you; / Whose will hath fashion'd all my thoughts anew" (II, iii,
100–101).

Mahomet has already been introduced by this point, since act
1, scene 2 had been given over to a conversation between him and
Alaham. Alaham had been infuriated with the counselor for his
part in convincing the king that Alaham's older (but half-witted)
brother Zophi should have primacy in the line of succession, and
now threatens him with death unless Mahomet kills Caine whom
Alaham knows to be Hala's lover. When Caine and Mahomet are

on stage together in the last scene of act 2, it becomes clear to both of them that they are caught in the middle and that there can be no satisfactory resolution for either.

Act 2 ends with a chorus of "Evil Spirits"—Malice, Craft, Pride, and Corrupt Reason—who survey the human condition and boast about their capacity to destroy man. If man chances from time to time to triumph over them, they care little, for they are confident of victory in the long run: "What need we haste? / Since till time ends, our raigne is sure to last." Act 1 had concluded with what theoretically should have been a balance to the "Evil Spirits," a chorus of "Good Spirits." And, it is true, the "Good Spirits" do present an ideal of human possibilities, or at least of human possibilities after death. While man is alive, they concede, he is apt to make the worst of his middle situation between animal and angel. As evidence of that tendency toward corruption they cite the examples of Alaham and Hala: "He makes wrong triumph over right, and innocence; / She makes her lust religions lord, confusion her defence" (61–62). The effect of the Chorus Primus is, then, anything but optimistic, an effect that is vehemently reinforced by the Chorus Secundus. With this sort of commentary on the action of the play, any possibility for moral grandeur on the part of the characters is severely limited.

Peter Ure has observed that the action of *Alaham* falls into two divisions, the first of which extends through act 3, scene 3.[13] This is the section of conspiratorial palace intrigue. In the first three scenes of act 3 the machinery that was set in motion in acts 1 and 2 continues to work. Alaham, prematurely boasting of his rank, vaults his power:

> I march above the wits, and hearts of men:
> Chance at my feet, and power in my hand.
> Now King indeed.
>
> (III, i, 13)

Having managed to bring about the deaths of both Mahomet and Caine, he confronts Hala with this news in act 3, scene 3. At first distraught by Caine's fate, she manages once again to dissemble and to vow loyalty to her husband as he moves forward.

With this news the second division of the play, the depiction of Hela's revenge, begins. As soon as Alaham leaves the stage, Hala allows her true feelings to erupt. Ostensibly directing her

statements at the Nutrix (nurse) who accompanies her, her real
audience is the abstraction of Rage:

> And is he gone? Rage then unprisoned be!
> I like thee well! While Alaham was there,
> Thou then didst use thy violence on me.
> Now prey abroad; swell above all respect.
>   (III, iv, 1–4)

She shocks the Nutrix with her plan to revenge Caine by killing
the child that she has had by Alaham. By the end of the scene she
has shifted her invocations to address yet another abstraction,
Caine's ghost:

> Open all lights of possibility;
> Let griefe, which yet keepes companie with death,
> Breake forth, and poyson all things with her breath.
>   (III, iv, 103–5)

Hala is nothing if she is not energetic and resourceful in her
search for vengeance, and she also tells the Nutrix of her devising
a poisoned crown and cloak for Alaham's coronation: "Glory now
at the Full is not suspitious; / And what addes to his pompe shall
him destroy" (III, iv, 87–88). Although seemingly melodramatic
in this brief summary, the scene nevertheless has a brutal power
that is properly shocking to a reader. Confronted by this manic
zeal, one can only be impressed by the creative spirit that brought
it into being.

   This scene has been singled out by Bullough as especially
crucial to the working-out of Greville's concept of tragedy in
Alaham in that it is here that the play's emphasis shifts firmly to
the female figure. Varthema's narrative that Greville used as a
source did not even mention the existence of the usurper's wife,
thereby remaining fully political in its orientation. But Greville
chooses to make this into a tragedy of sex as well as of politics.[14]
Hala now begins to control the plot and in so doing turns the play
decisively in the direction of classical drama depicting passionate
conflict between man and woman—in the direction, for example,
of the story of Aegisthus and Clytemnestra.

   There is one additional brief scene in act 3 presenting a relatively unimportant conversation between Hala and a priest
before Greville closes the act with the thematically crucial

Chorus Tertius. The chorus is written in the same ungainly poulter's measure of rhymed couplets of alternative twelve- and fourteen-syllable lines that Greville had used in the Chorus Primus, but there is a grave excitement to the passage that more than compensates for its metrical deficiencies. Set in the form of a debate between good and evil spirits, the speakers of the first two choruses here have the opportunity to confront one another directly with their differing world views. In light of what has happened in the play up to this point, the evil spirits obviously have a stronger evidentiary case, and they lose no time in taking advantage of it. Any belief in man's inherent goodness is folly, they taunt the good spirits. From the Garden of Eden where supposed virtue was in fact only "poore simplicity" onward, man has consistently manifested his tendencies toward corruption. Therefore, urge the evil spirits, the good spirits should "strive no more to carry men against affections streames" (44). The instances of Alaham and Hala show that they, the forces of Hell, are clearly in control: "We only make things cheape, or deare, as Lords of life, and death" (60). To this, the good spirits can respond only that in the long run virtue will triumph. In the meantime, the evil spirits will have to be allowed to "play here [i.e., on earth] with your art." From the perspective of eternity, the actions of the evil spirits will turn out to be counterproductive: "And so prove to the good but like those showres of raine, / Which, while they wet the husbandman, yet multiply his gaine" (107–8).

Such an attitude is cool comfort to anyone hoping for happiness in this life, but such nevertheless is the conclusion toward which the first three choruses of Alaham point. Greville would seem to want to enforce the concept not only of the existence of evil in human affairs but also of its certain triumph on earth. The events in the play that lead the reader to this conclusion are, we might suppose, reflective in some sense of the events that Greville had experienced in life.

At the opening of act 4, we meet the king's daughter Celica, and for a few scenes hope flares that good might at last have its day. True to her heavenly name, she speaks only of virtue and the highest of values. Her first discussion is with her tired, cowardly father, and she tries to give him backbone to resist Alaham for the good of the country. She then consoles her condemned brother Zophi, telling him that there is no escape except into the arms of God. Finally, face to face with her brother Alaham who insults her and threatens her before ordering her to be tortured and killed, she delivers herself of some very otherworldly statements and prepares herself to begin "eternall life." Taken in isolation, her speeches in this, her final, scene cannot help but seem a bit cloying, although apparently Greville wants an even more negative reaction toward her, since the capsule evaluation of her character in the prologue provides no basis for pity:

> Death in her fathers murther she affects,
> Seduc'd by glory; whose excesse still feedes
> It selfe, upon the barren steepes of mone.

In her histrionic self-pitying, we are to find her as vainglorious as the other characters.

Celica, Zophi, and the king are not, then, as obviously and actively wicked as Alaham and Hala, but neither do they possess the combination of strength and principle necessary to set matters right within themselves and within the state. There are strong indications that Mahomet might have emerged as a genuinely admirable man, but he is killed at the play's midpoint. Given this absence of opposition, Alaham and Hala continue to alternate having their own way (or, rather, *thinking* that they are having their own way) until the catastrophe of the last scene. Having done away with Mahomet, Caine, the king, Zophi, and Celica and having had all but Mahomet burned on the same funeral pyre, Alaham experiences first wild elation and then a "fall of spirits" (V, ii, 76), as the man who had seemed to be without conscience at last succumbs to the sensation of having his entrails torn by the ghosts of the dead. In the play's final scene he dons the crown and mantle Hala has prepared for him and the poison works its planned effect. As he dies, he is subjected to the further torture of his wife's fiendish jeers and her description of how she will murder their child in front of him before he expires. Ignoring his pleas to spare the infant, she proceeds with her plan, regretting only that the baby dies so quickly that she has no chance to feel fully revenged:

> Ah curst Mortality! So soone put out?
> And have I lost the glory of Revenge. . . ?
> Flesh is too brittle mould for brave excesse.
>   (V, iii, 90–91, 96)

But she too is soon brought up short when she discovers that in her passion and haste she has mistakenly killed the baby that she had by Caine. Nothing she can do now can reverse the error, and in a speech renouncing all hold on life, she condemns herself to Hell where her commitment to lust, fury, rage, and desire can be as permanent and excessive as she has always longed for it to be. Although not yet there physically, she has brought hell to herself spiritually.

While in some respects overwritten, this scene and others in *Alaham* are certainly capable of arousing a sense of terror that few earlier tragedians could equal. Greville's power as a controller of human emotion is not to be undervalued.

IV Mustapha

It cannot be established with certainty just when Greville, the habitual reviser, returned to work on the version of *Mustapha* that he had written in the mid-1590s. Bullough shows that it must have been at some point in the decade between 1604 and 1614, and Rebholz suggests 1607–1610 as the likely period.[15] It would not be surprising if the pirated edition of 1609 had something to do with his decision to rework and improve the play.

While he directed much of his attention to the choruses of the play, relocating them and expanding them, he also rewrote several speeches, changing their thematic development somewhat. The net effect of the changes shows *Mustapha* to be a clear advancement for Greville over what he had achieved in *Alaham*, a superiority that, in some respects, even the earlier version of the play shared. The dramatic conflicts in *Mustapha* are simultaneously clearer and more subtle than they were in *Alaham*, and the play avoids the structural weaknesses of the suddenly disappearing character (Mahomet) and the suddenly appearing character (Celica) that mar *Alaham*. The play gives its characters nearly as many opportunities for passionate ranting as does *Alaham*, and there is the same clear distinction made in most instances between the energies of good and evil. What chiefly distinguishes *Mustapha* as a drama is the presence of Achmat, the royal counselor. With his complex, self-divided mind, he perfects the kind of role that Mahomet had begun in *Alaham*. As an advisor to the king, he holds a position of great responsibility to the welfare of the state, but with an imperfect monarch as ruler, he is constantly uncertain as to how that welfare can best be maintained.

Like *Alaham*, *Mustapha* is partially a domestic tragedy centered on the conflicting passions of a husband and wife, although there are also strong political implications to the action that give the drama considerable stature as a document on the nature of human social organization. Both strains are present in the opening scene, a conversation between Soliman, emperor of Turkey, and Rossa, his wife and stepmother to the heir apparent Prince Mustapha. Clearly Rossa has planted seeds of suspicion of Mustapha's loyalty in Soliman's mind before the play opens, since in his first speech he is already acknowledging to her that he has perhaps misjudged his son's motives, vowing to exercise more control over him now lest he pose a threat to the security of Soliman's throne. What Rossa does not tell Soliman is that her intention in discrediting Mustapha is to improve the chances for succession to the throne of her own son Zanger. Her control over her husband is immense; he admits as much, but he attributes it not to any peculiarity in his own character so much as to a tendency in those men of his rank: "But love is onely that which Princes covet; / And for they have it least, they most doe love it" (I, i, 75–76). Even at this early point in the play, the reader recognizes how sadly mistaken Soliman is if he thinks that "love" is the best term for her sentiment for him.

As a ruler vacillating between tyranny and weakness, Soliman cannot fully engage one's sympathies. We might occasionally pity him or applaud him when he takes a position that we know to be morally right, but we are always aware also of his proclivity to back away from any decision that Rossa does not want him to make. To his credit, he tries in act 1, scene 2 to think more charitably of Mustapha than he has in the previous scene, supposing that the fickleness of "light humours" in men in general are even more prevalent in him as king: "If thus it worke in Man, much more in Thrones, / Whose tender heights feele all thinne aires that move" (I, ii, 21–22). But rather than making the obvious connection between his suspicions of his son and his wife, he instead supposes that the campaign to besmirch Mustapha is directed by Rosten, the husband of his daughter Camena. If this is indeed the case, Soliman muses, then the reports on Mustapha that he has been receiving from the Beglerby, a court official, must be correct. The Beglerby has been unequivocal in his praise of the emperor's son as a perfect prince:

> He windes not spirits up with Power, or Feare:
> The antient forms he keepes, where it is good:
> His projects reformation every where:
> His care to have diseases understood.
>
> (I, ii, 134–37)

On this information, Soliman decides not to follow the implicit
advice of Rossa to execute Mustapha:

> And shall I helpe to make succession lesse,
> Blasting the births of Nature and Example,
> In narrow feares of Selfe-unworthinesse?
>
> (I, ii, 230–32)

Saying that he will have new self-confidence is, of course, a different matter from actually having it, as Soliman's later actions
tragically demonstrate.

The Chorus Primus at the end of act 1 is heavily political in its
nature. Spoken by the "Bashas or Cadis" (counselors or judges), it
serves as an analysis of the kind of political corruption that Rossa
practices in the play itself. The Bashas are schemers by nature,
working, as they explain, in that crucial area of jurisdiction between monarch and people. Cynical about themselves as well as
about their society, they perceive laws only "as Sophistries of
every Common-weale" (58). They weave them to suit their needs,
and they are perfectly willing to accept the existence of tyranny as
long as their own desires are satisfied. They indict themselves
mercilessly for helping to deprive men of "Natures freedom."
Their final crime is one of sacrilege; in their corruption they "suffer God to wayne, / Under the Humors of a Sultans raigne"
(219–20).

The Chorus Primus provides a highly relevant transition to the
soliloquy of Achmat, the emperor's chief counselor, that opens act
2. Whatever the majority of the Bashas might be, it is clear from
Achmat's opening lines that he is quite the opposite. A man
dedicated to the principles of loyal service to the established
government, he is now distraught by what he sees happening
around him. Knowing the truth of Rossa's conniving, he
recognizes also the flaws in Soliman that have allowed the situation to deteriorate as far as it has. "I sworne am to my King, and
to his Honor: / His Humors? No" (II, i, 58–59), he concludes. He
realizes that in trying to influence Soliman in this sensitive matter

he runs the risk of losing credibility, but he sees no alternative to trying to preserve Mustapha: "I first am Natures subject, then my Princes; / I will not serve to Innocencies ruine" (II, i, 75–76).

When Soliman enters to Achmat, the emperor is no longer benign in his view of his son but has once again reverted to perceiving him as an upstart glory seeker who "shall die." His choice, as he understands it, is between whatever affection he might feel for Mustapha as his son and his obligations toward his country to provide stable, proper government:

> Practise, Ambition, Pride, are here disguised.
> And shall Love be a chaine, tyed to my Crowne,
> Either to helpe him up, or pull me downe?
> No, no: This Father-language fits not Kings,
> Whose publike, universall providence
> Of Things, not Persons, alwayes must have sense.
> With Justice I these misty doubts will cleare.
> And he that brakes divine, and humane Law,
> Shall no protection out of either draw.
>
> (II, ii, 35–43)

It is a particularly crucial speech in the play because, as Rebholz has observed, Soliman here betrays the inability of his mind to understand the roles of acting as a king and acting as a father as being anything but mutually exclusive.[16] In thinking that he has to kill his son in order to save the state, he confuses the workings of worldly institutions with what Greville would have called the divinely ordained relationship between father and son. Achmat tries to draw his attention to the existence of this higher law: "Yet Solyman! let Feare awake Kings counsells. / But feare not Natures lawes, which seldome alter" (II, ii. 93–94). But he can win no more than another temporary pause from Soliman who blindly persists in thinking that he will preserve his nation when, in fact, as Rebholz again notes, the violence of his unnatural act only sets a precedent for those who, at the end of the play, want to overthrow the established order.[17]

Unlike *Alaham*, where only the two central characters possessed real dramatic interest, several of the secondary characters in *Mustapha* are subtly and carefully developed. In Camena, Soliman and Rossa's daughter, we see someone who, though in a small role, has the same sort of wrenching conflict of loyalties as do more important characters. When she enters the play in act 2,

scene 3, she informs the reader in a soliloquy that her ties to her
father, to her mother, to her husband Rosten, to her brother
Zanger, and to her half-brother Mustapha have rendered her virtually impotent, emotionally and morally:

> Truth bids me runne, by Truth I am retired;
> Shame leades me both the one way, and the other.
> In what a Labyrinth is Honor cast,
> Drawne diverse wayes with Sex, with Time, with State?
>   (II, iii, 25–28)

In speaking with her father, however, she musters the strength to
plead quite fervently on Mustapha's behalf, and, in so doing, she
aligns herself with what are clearly the forces of right in the play.

The interest that the reader develops in Camena and in Achmat
is to a considerable extent attributable to Greville's emphasizing
the empathetic qualities in their natures. One's interest in someone like Rossa is, on the other hand, more the product of fascination in an extreme of the human personality. A third kind of
character—one who serves principally as the expositor of a certain philosophic position—is exemplified by the priest and the
Beglerby who in act 4, scene 4 are brought on stage to offer their
views of Mustapha's fate. The Beglerby stands aside, unseen by
the priest and Mustapha, until the very end of the scene. The
Beglerby, in this scene and in the others in which he appears, is
consistently presented as a fairly corrupt and cynical timeserver,
someone who can say with complete nonchalance that "The Saint
we worship is Authoritie; / Which lives in Kings, and cannot
with them die" (IV, iv, 17–18) and who in his next breath can
dismiss Mustapha as merely a "Foot–ball to the Starres":
"Whether he get the Crowne, or lose his blood, / The one is ill to
him; to me both good" (IV, iv, 30–31). The priest, as representative of God's church, is not much better, however, since he
recognizes the ways in which he too has been compromised by ex-
posure to and participation in the exercise of temporal power:

> O wretched Flesh! in which must be obeyed
> Gods law, that wills Impossibilitie;
> And Princes wills, the gulfes of Tyrannie.
> We Priests, even with the mysterie of words,
> First binde our selves, and with our selves the rest

> To servitude, the sheath of Tyrants sword;
> Each worst unto himselfe, approving best.
>
>   (IV, iv, 38–44)

But at least his conscience is troubled by what he has done:

> I Mustapha have ruin'd, and this State.
> I am the Evills friend, Hells Mediator,
> A Furie unto man, a man to Furies.
>
>   (IV, iv, 53–55)

This happens to be the only scene in which Mustapha appears, and he emerges as a perfect foil to the other two men who are on stage with him. He is otherworldly in the extreme, caring little what happens to him in this life, since one alternative is as tainted by mortality and therefore as painful as another:

> Since therefore Life is but the throne of Woe,
> Which sicknesse, paine, desire, and feare inherit,
> Ever most worth to men of weakest spirit:
> Shall we, to languish in this brittle Jayle,
> Seeke, by ill deeds, to shunne ill destinie?
> And so, for toyes, lose immortalitie?
>
>   (IV, iv, 133–38)

The entirety of the play makes it clear that indeed men like Mustapha *are* out of place in the world, but their attitudes are nevertheless infinitely preferable to those of the Beglerby and the priest.

The organization of *Mustapha* is perfectly linear. Greville arranges his scenes so that each serves as a successively further point in Soliman's succumbing to vanity and fear, giving up the royal strength he originally had and moving toward the killing of his son, an act which is reported by Achmat in act 5, scene 2. At two points, however, the action slows to permit us closer views of Soliman and Rossa in moments of relative introspection. Rossa has her turn first, in act 3, scene 1, where she describes to her son-in-law Rosten what has gone right and what wrong with her strategies to this point. She is more arrogant and defiant here than we have previously seen her to be, and she ends the scene with an explicit vow of her own malevolence:

> My chiefest End
> Is, first to fix the World on my Succession;
> Next so to alter, plant, remove, create,
> That I, not he, may fashion this Estate.
>   (III, i, 150–53)

Soliman's parallel scene is the opening of act 4, where, after praying, he receives a terrible vision of horrors and disorder to come if he kills Mustapha. But surprisingly, rather than yielding to what is apparently the clear will of heaven, he persists in his worldly campaign of violence:

> The Earth drawes one way, and the skie another.
> If God worke thus, Kings must looke upwards still,
> And from these Powers they know not, choose a will.
> Or else beleeve themselves, their strength, occasion;
> Make wisdome conscience; and the world their skie:
> So have all Tyrants done; and so must I.
>   (IV, i, 38–43)

Opting for tyranny and rationalizing the decision with the shaky logical claim that previous tyrants have made the same choice, Soliman here seals his fate. There now will be no more vacillation.

Two further speeches are deserving of some attention: the final anguished cries of Rossa and the moody ruminations of Achmat that directly precede them. Rossa, like Hala in *Alaham*, is given the closing speech in the play. As was the case in the other drama, Greville's decision to assign the speech to the leading female character is indicative of his desire to invest these women with the grandeur of their ancestors in classical drama. But a comparison of Rossa's speech with Hala's cannot help but lead to the conclusion that Rossa's is the weaker. True, the notes struck in the diatribes are much the same: lust, anger, defiance. Rossa, however, never attains the black limits of nihilism that does Hala. Her end is quieter, even though she does not want it to be so.

One further reason for the relative lack of power of Rossa's speech is that it immediately follows Achmat's observations on the state of affairs in the realm, and the interest generated by his ideas cannot help but detract from what Rossa says. His speech is the culmination of the internal debate that he has carried on with himself throughout the play regarding the issue of his continuing to counsel and support a monarch whom he knows to be morally bankrupt. Greville revised this scene rather extensively in the later version of the play to sharpen the dilemma confronting Achmat and to make his decision more dramatic. Achmat knows that a popular revolt has already begun as a result of public outrage over Mustapha's death, and Achmat must now decide whether he should aid this revolt against a tyrant or continue to serve Soliman for the sake of the stability of the state. With half his mind he wants to side with the people, as he urges them to "Proceed in Furie: Furie hath Law, and Reason, / Where it doth plague the wickednesse of Treason" (V, iii, 96–97). But the other half of his mind pulls him back from such a course: "But stay! Shall Man the Damme, and Grave of Crownes, / With Mutinie, pull sacred Scepters downe?" (V, iii, 102–3). The sovereign must prevail over the people, he feels, and so therefore he will do what he can, at great personal risk, to prop up the unstable government:

> No. Achmat! Rather, with thy hazard, strive
> To save this high rais'd Soveraignitie,
> Under whose wings there was an Prosperitie.
> (V, iii, 112–14)

An essentially decent man consciously choosing to support a tyrant is not, of course, a pleasant thing to watch, but Greville provides the reader with two mitigating factors. First, Achmat *does* have much to say in support of rebellion, and even if he eventually decides not to side with the rebels, his words remain to echo in the reader's mind. Second, Greville brings Achmat back on stage once more in the final scene as a nearly silent witness to the agony of Rossa. In this, there is at least an ironic poetic justice.

A consideration of Achmat's quandary serves as a reminder that, in several respects, *Mustapha* is a distinctly political play. This political dimension emerges most clearly in the choruses that follow each act. When Greville revised the play, his decision to rearrange and expand the choruses had the effect of making them less plausible dramatically but no doubt more consistent with his view of the drama as a philosophical exposition and debate. The political nature of the Chorus Primus, spoken by the Turkish Bashas, has already been noted. The Chorus Secundus, absent in the early version of the play, is similarly assigned to a group of local speakers, Mahomedan Priests. Starting their 210-line speech in stanzas of six lines each, they switch at line 120 to rhymed couplets. Such changes are not unusual in Greville who often is willing to abandon a chosen verse form if it seems to be getting in the way of his thought. The priests touch on a sizable number of topics in the chorus, contrasting martial nations with artistic, contemplative nations, describing various relationships between the church and the monarch, and comparing the overt tyranny of Turkey with the more subtle (and, they feel, more pernicious) ways of manipulating laws in Christian countries. According to them, Western governments practice

> An Art by which Man seemes, but is not free;
> Crownes keeping all their specious guiding reynes,
> Fast in the hand of strong Authority.
>
> (115–17)

But again, before we suppose that Greville is antimonarchical in his sympathies, we need to notice the careful modulation away from the attitude embodied in these lines toward a yet more generalized conclusion that places responsibility for governmental ills not on the rulers but on the sinful men that they rule:

> Whence I conclude: Mankinde is both the Forme,
> And Matter, wherewith Tyrannies transforme:
> For Power can neither see, worke, or devise,
> Without the Peoples hands, hearts, wit, and eyes:
> So that were Man not by himselfe opprest,
> Kings would not, Tyrants could not make him beast.
>
> (205–10)

This idea of man's essentially errant nature is reiterated in the Chorus Tertius, a dialogue between Time and Eternity. The debate was a familiar one in the Renaissance, and Greville organizes the issues in this chorus so that little comfort is to be found in the positions taken by either concept. Time, who might be thought to be more closely attuned to man's problems, is in fact very cool in his attitude toward man's difficulties: "The Earth is mine: of earthly things the care / I leave to Men, that like them, earthly are" (47–48). He wants no blame attached to him for mistakes made by "Mans still-erring will" (70): "Shall I, that in my selfe still golden am, / By their Grosse metall, beare an Iron name?" (71–72). Eternity, in his speech, addresses Time

principally, but his argument is obliquely directed at man, whom
he considers to be Time's creature. He finishes on a very lofty
note, inviting Time to do whatever he wants to do, assuring him
that he, Eternity, will remain serenely indifferent: "Doe what
you can: Mine shall subsist by Me: / I am the measure of
Felicitie" (149–50). The possibility for human consolation here
would seem to be nil.

The Chorus Quartus of converts to Mahomedanism continues
to pursue the theme of decline and fall. First the angels fell, then
man. Man's institutions, especially the church and the empire,
have steadily deteriorated since their inception. Originally the
monarch and the church were mutually supportive, but in later
times they divide and oppose one another. With this collapse
comes chaos:

> So in that Noble worke of publike Government,
> When Crownes, Church, Souldiers, or the Lawes
>   doe overmuch dissent,
> That frame, wherein they liv'd, as fatally, dissolv'd.
> And each in gulfes of selfe-Conceipt, as fatally,
>   involv'd.
>
> (103–6)

It is no surprise that men will revolt against such corrupt leaders.
The only surprise is that these speakers converted to the cause of
organized religion at all.

The early version of *Mustapha* had ended without any chorus,
but the posthumous text of 1633 has two, a chorus of Tartars and
a closing Chorus Sacerdotum of priests. Both had appeared at
earlier points in the play in the first version—the Chorus Tartarorum at the end of act 3 and the Chorus Sacerdotum at the end
of act 1—but Greville apparently wanted them to stand here at
the close where they could simultaneously oppose and complement one another. The Chorus Tartarorum distills all that is present elsewhere in the play that is critical of superstitious religion.
The qualifier "superstitious" is important here because the chorus
itself uses the word twice in emphatic positions; it is true that *no*
kind of religion receives their praise, but unsuperstitious faith
does at least escape their attack. In opposition to the false religion
that they believe has led Mustapha to choose death over life, they
set "Nature" whom they say encourages self-preservation and, in-

deed, aggressiveness. Theirs is a naturalism of pure worldliness, unalloyed by any belief in supernatural powers.

The Chorus Sacerdotum is one of Greville's most anthologized passages, and its analysis of the human situation in terms of the difficulty of mortal man's living by immortal laws is extraordinarily striking:

> Oh wearisome Condition of Humanity!
> Borne under one Law, to another bound.
>   (1–2)

Outside the context from which it is taken, the twenty-four line chorus seems to be a passage of stoicism spoken by priests who can only struggle with a religion that remains enigmatic to them:

> We that are bound by vowes, and by Promotion,
> With pompe of holy Sacrifice and rites,
> To teach beleefe in good and still devotion,
> To preach of Heavens wonders, and delights:
> Yet when each of us, in his owne heart lookes,
> He findes the God there, farre unlike his Bookes.
>   (19–24)

Taken, however, as the final word in a play which has had much to say about the relative claims of Heaven and Earth, most recently in the Chorus Tartarorum, this chorus reiterates the kind of dilemma which several of the characters have faced. When, for example, in act 4, scene 4, the Beglerby and the priest explained their beliefs, it was done very much in just these terms. The priest in that scene clearly wanted to believe, but could not abandon the claims of the world with their concomitant pressures for unbelief. So these priests of the chorus find themselves tormented by the nature to which the Tartars have given in. The priests want to find the "waies to good" (18), but they have come to realize that as long as they are living within nature that will be impossible. It is tempting to say, as Joan Rees has done, that Greville is speaking through this chorus in his own voice, that he characteristically identifies with these priests (and with Achmat) who would love to rise above the perils of the world but who instead are constantly pulled back by the "wearisome Condition of Humanity."[18] But the priests finally are hypocrites, teaching something in which they cannot believe. And Greville, however far-reaching his skep-

tical doubts, seems usually to have been able to make the leap of
faith that eludes these characters.

V   *Greville as Dramatist*

In the limited amount of criticism that has been written on
Greville's plays, two approaches have developed, opposite in
nature. The first emphasizes the political and philosophical
nature of the dramas and concentrates heavily on the choruses as
being most representative of Greville's somber, tragic world
view.[19] The second approach, developed most explicitly by Peter
Ure, places far more emphasis on the development of the
characters within the plays, on what Ure chooses to describe as
Greville's extensive explorations of the "inward man."[20] Both approaches have something valuable to contribute to our understanding of Greville, but either can, in isolation, give a rather un-
balanced view of Greville's achievement. It would seem only
reasonable to pay attention both to the specification of the
characters' inward lives as they provide such specification in their
speeches and to the more generalized comment that the choruses
make on the characters' situations, comment that often manifests
an interesting bias of its own. This last notion needs especially to
be stressed lest the reader think that the choruses are to be taken
as expressions of Greville's own attitudes toward their subjects. It
is quite possible—in fact, likely—that in some of them Greville's
opinions *do* coincide with his speakers', although probably not
nearly to the extent that some critics have maintained. To claim
that there *is* such a continuing coincidence is to encounter
numerous critical muddles when it is discovered that the choruses
contradict one another. Rather, as Bullough cautioned years ago,
we must notice that Greville thought of the speakers of his
choruses as particular groups of people and made determined efforts to keep what they say "in character."[21] When read with this
in mind, the plays can become far more balanced dramatic
wholes.

A concentration on Greville's ability to develop character takes
one in the direction of most modern criticism of Renaissance
drama. Approaching Greville from this perspective can only, in
spite of Ure's efforts, have the effect of making Greville into an
inferior dramatist when compared with the more well-known
playwrights of the Renaissance popular stage. Tourneur or

Webster, to say nothing of Shakespeare, simply know how to handle characters far more adroitly than Greville does.

Greville fares much better when compared to the dramatists who wrote for the private theaters. His plays would not be that much more unmanageable on stage than would the tragedies of Chapman or Marston, and the intellectual content of his drama is unsurpassed in the English Renaissance.[22] Bullough thinks that "the only Elizabethan who approached the grandeur of his conceptions was Shakespeare," although, he goes on, "except occasionally he lacked the power of dramatic projection, and even more important, of quickening words."[23] That this is so, and I agree that it is so, is unfortunate, for in his plays Greville reveals those sides of his mind that make him one of the most fascinating thinkers of his age. If only he had been able to create plays that were more convincing *as drama* he would not have to be relegated to the rear ranks of Elizabethan playwrights. As matters stand, we can only lament the curious combination of drama that is at once too stylized and too personal. Greville doubtlessly does reveal his own passions and sentiments on vital issues in oblique ways in these plays. But he has trouble channeling these sentiments into the stiff form of Senecan dialogue. He is far more comfortable with the relative freedom of the lyric, as the final poems of *Caelica* clearly show.

CHAPTER 4

The Philosopher

WHILE Greville's five long poems ("treaties," to use his word for them) can hardly strike the modern reader as anything but curiosities, the Renaissance produced several such efforts. For that matter, there are sizable stretches of discursive philosophy set into verse in almost any of the long narrative poems of the period; the *Faerie Queene* is an obvious example. But the genre of the long philosophical poem was distinct from the others, and it is this form, more than any other, that has failed to survive. Although the type did live on into the eighteenth century in poems such as Pope's *Essay on Man* and Johnson's *Vanity of Human Wishes*, it was in Greville's own era that the verse treatise flourished with special hardiness. Sir John Davies' *Orchestra* and *Nosce Teipsum*, George Chapman's *Euthymiae Raptus; or The Teares of Peace*, and Samuel Daniel's *Musophilus* (dedicated to Greville) are but a few examples of poetic expressions of Christian humanist philosophy written during the same period in which Greville was at work on his treatises. While some of these poems attracted little attention, others were notably popular; *Nosce Teipsum* went through six editions in twenty-five years.

Not all philosophy, to be sure, was set forth in verse—Richard Hooker's *Of the Laws of Ecclestical Polity* and Sir Francis Bacon's *Essays* are two obvious examples of the period's finest prose—but it is nevertheless true that a writer would have perceived poetry as an entirely appropriate vehicle for the expression of complex systems of ideas. When Greville began his treatises he had probably tried one lengthy piece of prose—the *Letter to an Honourable Lady*—but he had also written the first versions of his dramas, and he had perhaps found that he prefered working with political and moral thought in the metrically patterned way in which he had handled them in the play's choruses. With but a few exceptions, the stanza of the treatises is the same six-line stanza

rhyming *a b a b c c* that he had used in several of the choruses. His
ability to handle this stanza with relative grace over the long haul
of the treatises is not the least of his achievements in the poems.

I *Subjects and Dates*

The poems' titles are quite accurate indications of the range of
subject matters. From the relatively practical and descriptive *A
Treatie of Warres* and *A Treatise of Monarchy* to the greater
abstraction of *A Treatie of Humane Learning, An Inquisition on
Fame and Honour*, and *A Treatise of Religion*, Greville am-
bitiously chooses to survey virtually all human activity. Bacon's
youthful boast of taking all knowledge as his province in effect receives a restatement in the poems of an aging statesman.

As usual in any discussion of Greville's canon, one must confess
uncertainty about the dates of the treatises. The latest opinion,
from Rebholz, sets *Monarchy* as the earliest poem, from the
period between 1599 and 1604 (or approximately the same time
as the dramas). Then, after a ten-year interval, Greville returned
to the idea of the treatise, and Rebholz thinks that, with the exception of the last four poems of *Caelica*, he wrote only the
treatises in the last stage of his career: *Fame and Honour* in
1612–1614, *Wars* in 1619–1621, *Human Learning* in 1620–1622,
and, finally, *Religion* in the years immediately preceding his
death in 1628.[1] The chief opposing views on dating are held by
Rees, who concludes her study with a refusal to come to any conclusion—to her way of thinking the dates of the treatises simply
cannot be determined[2]—and by Bullough, who would place
Monarchy at the end of the list rather than at the beginning.
Aside from a few allusions which he thinks indicate a later rather
than an earlier date, he argues his case for a late date mainly on
the grounds of style. The bare, prosaic style of *Monarchy* must,
he feels, place the poem in Greville's final phase when he had
come to distrust anything ornamental in its nature.[3] The issue
seems beyond any satisfactory resolution, but my choice is to
follow Rebholz, believing as I do that the style of *Monarchy* is one
that Greville could have adopted at any point in his career and
that, beyond arguments about evidence, we can best develop
possibilities for tracing certain themes from treatise to treatise by
discussing *Monarchy* first.

It should also be noted that the issue of dating the treatises is made no easier by the fact that two of them, *Monarchy* and *Religion*, were not included in the posthumous edition of 1633 but instead had to await separate publication in 1670 as *The Remains of Sir Fulk Grevill Lord Brooke*. It is clear from a comment in Greville's hand in the manuscript of the treatises that Greville wanted *Religion* to come first in any collected edition:

> These treatises should be thus placed.
> 1. Religion.
> 2. Humane Learninge.
> 3. Fame & Honor.
> 4. Warre.

And it seems likely that Greville's literary executor did in fact intend to follow Greville's ordering since the 1633 edition has the last three in their prescribed order, and there is clear textual evidence that *Religion* was intended for publication in the volume prior to the treatise's suppression by an official censor, probably because of its antiprelatical nature.[4]

Greville's arrangement for the treatises makes thematic sense from one point of view, for it places the poems in descending order of importance for their author. There can be no doubt as to Greville's feelings on the primacy of religion among these subjects. It provides the philosophical base vital to an understanding of the progressively narrowing focus of the following three poems. Yet, Greville's ordering of the poems cannot call attention to other mutations of attitudes and themes as can a chronological arrangement. A reading of the poems in what I am supposing to be the order of their composition shows a progression in Greville's opinions on the dual nature of human existence, from a greater interest in affairs of the world in *Monarchy* to a denial of the value of worldliness in *Religion*, where it is clear that he is willing to set aside all effort in mundane affairs as valueless when compared with the overwhelming urgency of the needs of the spirit.

II A Treatise of Monarchy

In the *Life of Sidney* Greville says that one section of this treatise. "The Declination of Monarchy," began as a modification of some of the choruses from the tragedies. It cannot be known what stages of development the poem went through on its way to

its final total of 664 stanzas divided into fifteen sections. The end
result is both the longest of the treatises and the most unique. The
metaphysical speculation that so characterizes the other treatises
is here relatively absent, as Greville focuses his attention principally on the functioning of monarchies, past and present. That
the poem was not included in the 1633 edition is perhaps an
understandable consequence of its descriptive frankness; a less
than dazzling Stuart regime could not have been particularly
comfortable with any detailed analysis of the nature of kingship,
even when that analysis had been carried out by such a thorough-
going monarchist as Greville.

The poem presents the reader with a greater challenge than
any of the other treatises, in part because of its analytical nature.
In attempting to cover virtually all aspects of the governance of
the realm, Greville runs the risk of becoming prosaic when working his way through subjects such as harbor-dredging and bridge-
building. But if large stretches of this perhaps overly long poem
fail to engage the aesthetic imagination, it is also true that other
sections, particularly at the opening and closing, concern
themselves in a thoughtful and sometimes moving way with some
of the fundamental issues of human social organization. Preferring always to describe what is or what has been or what might
be, Greville provides in this treatise a statement of English
Renaissance *realpolitik*. Aligning himself thus more in the tradition of Machiavelli than of Hooker, whose *Laws* had been far
more theoretical than practical, he works toward a codification
of the means by which a monarchy might be made to operate
most effectively.

The two opening sections provide an historical perspective for
the rest of the poem. In section 1, "Of the Beginning of Monarchy," he establishes a causal relationship between the present
state of monarchy and the fallen nature of man. In a prelapsarian
golden world, ideal man lived in happy union with ideal, semi-
divine kings: "For in those goulden dayes, with natures
chaines / Both Kinge, and people seem'd conjoyn'd in one"(st.
2).[5] But as the golden age came to an end, as the gods withdrew
from the world to a far more remote distance from men, as men
were forced to find kings from among themselves, and as men
became more aware of their own corruption, monarchy came increasingly to be a flawed human institution. In his description of
this process of the establishing of the modern concept of kingship,

Greville takes a slightly ambiguous stance on one of the principal theoretical aspects of the subject, the nature of the power transferred from people to monarch at the moment in which a king is chosen. Earlier apologists of absolutism such as Jean Bodin had insisted that *all* power was given to the monarch in perpetuity when such a government was established. The absolutist point of view provoked sharp opposition in print, most notably from George Buchanan, writing prior to Greville, and John Milton, writing forty-five years later, both of whom were persuaded that any assignment of power to the monarch was revocable by those being ruled at any time that they saw fit.[6]

Greville's preference in this argument is in general for the absolutist position. It was, he says, out of necessity that men first acted to create a monarch, and that necessity seems still to exert its force on the present:

> And scorning equalls, raise a Soveraigne must:
> For frailty with it self growen discontent.
> Ward-like must lyve in others government.
>
> (st. 24)

It is fruitless now to try to change the terms of the agreement. The monarch's subjects must simply accept their inferior status:

> Man then repyne not at these boundless kinges,
> Since yow endure the fate of your forefathers,
> To whome God did foretell, on humane winges
> How inequality once rais'd, still gathers;
> Their choice offended him, please you it must,
> Whose dreggs still in you, on you make it just.
>
> (st. 25)

This is cool comfort indeed for an unhappy nation, although Greville does have something warmer to offer in the following stanza:

> Princes againe ore'rack not your creation,
> Least power returne to that whence it began;
> But keepe upp scepters by that reputation
> Which raised one, to rule this world of man:
> Order makes us the body, you the head,
> And by disorder anarchie is bred.
>
> (st. 26)

The monarch must recognize that he must rule for his people's good, although the reason given for doing so is not so much the intrinsic rights of the people as it is the stability of the state. To rule despotically is to invite rebellion and anarchy, a fate that in Greville's view is the worst that can befall a kingdom. The three-stanza passage goes far in summing up Greville's view of what the proper condition of a nation should be. It clearly is not a particularly blissful state of existence; there is more for all parties to endure than there is for them to enjoy. It is, however, a stable society with at least minimal liberties for all. And that, as one learns from almost all of Greville's works, is all he feels man has a right to expect.

Working as he does from the premise of the fallen nature of man and monarch alike, Greville the monarchist has a good deal to say about the weaknesses of all monarchies. All too often, kings have tried to exploit religion to secure their power (a theme from both of the plays), but "true religions cleare beames" (st. 40) will expose this duplicity whenever the observer will allow it to do so. Tyranny, however, has had its way in a regrettable number of instances where the "excesses of a Crowne" (st. 45) have suppressed opposition. In titling his second edition "Declination of Monarchy to Violence," Greville begins rehearsing specific examples of monarchial privilege abused. Mahomet, Cambyses, Caracalla, the pope (presumably any pope will do), all have shown themselves to be degenerate rulers, and their flaws of ego should serve as negative examples for all responsible kings.

Some monarchs have, in Greville's opinion, been guilty of errors deriving from the opposite failing, from a royal weakness that serves only to confuse the kingdom. Sections 3 and 4 of *Monarchy* take up this flaccidity in some rulers and suggest ways of counteracting it. The weak king, it is said, should at least recognize his weakness so that he will be able to prevent others' taking advantage of it. Since, for example, a weak king's favorites have often been able to manipulate him, Greville counsels a prudent choice of advisors, a careful balancing of one faction against another so that royal power remains supreme. What Greville does not acknowledge is the fact that any king with the sagacity to pursue such a course would not in all likelihood be weak in the first place.

Still, the more probable threat to a nation's well-being is apt to come from a domineering ruler, and it is to this subject of "strong

tyrants" that Greville devotes the fifth section of the poem.
Greville rarely finds fault with strength as such, only with some
excesses that often accompany strength. The fame and reputation
of a strong leader are indeed things to be admired; they are part
of "the beauty of authoritie" (st. 159). But a monarch must take
care lest "extortions, crueltie, oppression, / Covetousnes, end-
lesse anger, or displeasure" (st. 161) detract from his more commendable qualities. If, however, the king *does* succumb to the
temptations of tryanny, if he does oppress his people, there is
little that they can do about it. Greville reformulates the position
that he has already taken in the first section:

> But if pow're will exceed, then lett mankinde
> Receave oppression, as fruites of their error;
> Let them againe live in their duties shrinde,
> As their safe haven from the windes of terror,
> > Till hee that rais'd powre, to mowe mans synnes downe,
> > Please, for pow'rs owne synnes, to pluck off her Crowne.
>
> (st. 191)

Only God may overthrow a tyrant; the people must accept tyranny as punishment for their sins. In taking these positions,
Greville is aligning himself rather closely with the doctrine of the
divine right of kings as propounded by both James I and his son
Charles I. Maclean observes that Greville by no means accepts all
of the Stuart doctrine,[7] but he does come close enough on the central issues such as this one that he must be counted among the political thinkers on whom James could most firmly rely for support.

While Greville considers the church to be the "first foundation
of government" (st. 202), he recognizes that "Church rites alone"
cannot organize society sufficiently (st. 246). Therefore, civil
laws are necessary that the monarch's reign might be effective.
The sovereign should not look on laws as encroachments upon his
power but rather as means for preventing his subjects from in-
truding to too great an extent into the source of that power. Laws
never seem to Greville to exist principally for the protection of
anyone's rights as much as they do to remind everyone of the

> mutuall duties to which man is borne;
> > And from which noe soule can deliverd be,
> > By tyme, discretion, or authoritie.
>
> (st. 240)

In responding to this natural and universal call of duty manifested in civil laws, all members of society cooperate to bring
about an effective social organization. Greville states most clearly
here what he has suggested elsewhere: that the king too is bound
by laws both divine and mortal.

> For actyve powre must not her bounds enlarge
> By stretching Crowne rights (which by law descend)
> To tax, impose, monopolize, or charge,
> As if both God, and mans law had no end.
>
> (st. 310)

Both the tyrant and the king can use laws, he says, but only the
king recognizes that the "publique cause" demands that the law
apply also to him. If James approved of what he found elsewhere
in *Monarchy*, it seems unlikely that he would have been encouraged by this point.

The final eight sections of the poem, especially sections 8
through 12, are certain to be of less interest. They survey various
aspects of government activity—commerce, crown revenue,
peace, war—and comment on what should and should not be
done in each domain. These sections can only strike the modern
reader (if not Greville's contemporaries) as bizarre examples of
poetry doing the work of prose. For his vision of a well-run
government, Greville is doubtlessly looking backward to the reign
of Elizabeth, an era that, throughout his later work, he consistently idealizes as the epitome of a harmonious, efficient state. He
had had enough reservations about the queen while she was still
alive, but now, in comparison with James, he finds her reign to be
nearly without flaw.

The last three sections of the poem return to a somewhat more
theoretical position, comparing the monarchical system of
government to government by an aristocracy and by democracy.
The purpose of the comparison is to establish the superiority of
monarchy to either of the two competing forms, and the method
of argument is once again from historical example. The fate of
Rome affords evidence of what happens when kings are abol-
ished. Rome struggled through what to Greville was the near
anarchy of the consuls, the decemvirs, the tribunes, and the
triumvirate until monarchy was reestablished in the emperors.
Where "manie heads" (st. 594) distribute rewards and enforce

justice no unanimity of national purpose can be established. The evils of such governments are only magnified when the basis for making decisions moves past aristocracy into democracy where "that blinde multitude chiefe Master is" (st. 610). Whatever prominence republican Rome or Athens might have enjoyed is said to be due to periods of strong, centralized control rather than to alternating periods of rule by the people. In a democracy, there can be no hope for permanence.

Permanence, order, stability: these finally are the qualities that Greville values most highly in government. In this, presumably, his first treatise, he is confident that man's innate reason will lead him to monarchy:

> And as we doe in humane bodies see,
> Where reason raignes in chiefe, not the affection,
> Order is greate, not wanton libertie,
> Man to himself, and others a direction.
>
> (st. 657)

He was to come eventually to lose much of his confidence in the powers of reason to guide men correctly, but at this point he has no cause to doubt his own, or his king's, wisdom.

III An Inquisition Upon Fame and Honour

Greville probably wrote this treatise near the end of his decade-long enforced retirement from government service. It would have been an appropriate moment for him to take up this theme in that his years of quiet, following as they did a youthful career in which fame had doubtless been an inspiring motive, would have been years given over in part to reflection upon what his life had amounted to thus far. The treatise clearly shows his recognition of the centrality of the theme in the thought of his age, of the desire for immortality achieved through public accomplishment that so attracted many of his contemporaries. Shakespeare in the *Sonnets* and Spenser in *The Ruines of Time*, to cite only two examples, ask to what extent virtuous action (including the writing of poetry) can transcend mortality. Bullough observes that two attitudes toward the subject had developed by the time that Greville took it up—the one an arrogant assurance that human creation could in fact conquer time and the other an elegaic wistfulness that no matter how impressive an act might be at the moment time would eventually wash it all away.[8]

In treating the topic, all of Greville's contemporaries proceed from the assumption that the pursuit of fame is essentially a proper, even a noble, activity for men; to them it is merely a question of how long-lasting the results of that activity can be. The presence of the word "inquisition" in the title of Greville's poem indicates, however, that he is working from a far more skeptical stance than were any of the lyric and elegaic poets. His is an analytical treatise that accepts nothing as true until rational examination has made it so, and while his poetry often enough shows him prone to psychological depression and even fear, he never gives himself over to the kind of sweet, nostalgic melancholy that had characterized some of the other treatments of the topic.

The first half of the eighty-six-stanza treatise is devoted to a survey of past views on fame and honor. There is little to surprise one here as Greville contents himself with repeating ideas that were part of the stock-in-trade of most Renaissance thinkers. He acknowledges immediately that honor has been the highest goal for man from the days of Hercules to the present. A necessary social and governmental incentive, it has served to bring worthy men into public service: "For else, what Governour would spend his dayes, / In envious travell, for the publike good?" (st. 7).[9] This is not to say that the pursuit of fame and honor (Greville, by the way, seems to use the terms interchangeably) perfects man or his institutions since they are all held to be corrupt, all have "subsistence failing, and unsteady" (st. 13), but it does seem to have kept the situation from deteriorating precipitously. At best, however, fame has to be seen as an external support to man and not as a genuine substitute for inner virtue: "Man, out of man, will make himselfe a frame, / Seekes outward helpe, and borrowes that of Fame" (st. 19).

Though he shares the beliefs of the Stoic philosophers from time to time, Greville has little use for their contention that one is better off retreating into himself than in pursuing the chimera of fame. This Stoic withdrawal he dismisses as mere "pride of thought" (st. 21). To the inactivity engendered by such attitudes he greatly prefers the "pride of deeds" which can help a nation forward and which must, in some measure, reflect more abstract concepts of virtue: "Yet from these grounds, if Fame wee over-throw, / We lose mans eccho, both of wrong and right"(st. 26).

This much having been said in defense of fame, Greville turns to an enumeration of its faults. Most importantly, it has nothing to do with the salvation of one's soul or to the "inward peace" that anticipates that salvation. Since "mans chiefe vertue, is Hu-militie" (st. 33), any pursuit of honor can only signal a turning away from higher spiritual priorities. To complement this Chris-tian, spiritual deficiency, Greville points to the intractability of fame in the public world from classical times to the present. Those who seek to be famous must deal with the fickleness of opinion, and one can never be sure where one stands in that endeavor. Fame is a "monster . . . never uniforme" (st. 53) so it is pointless to attempt to control it.

The cause of the search for fame and honor is identified as the deadliest of the seven deadly sins, pride. Nine stanzas, 60 through 68, are given over to an analysis of the ways in which pride cor-rupts man's already-marred nature so as to send him off in pursuit of "applause, and selfe-opinion" (st. 65). But pride leads almost inevitably, in this case and in other human frailties in which it has a part, to despair when the thing in which one took pride evaporates. Fame is "hard gotten" and "worse to keepe" (st. 71).

Greville recognizes that in this rebuttal of fame he is working himself into a contradiction of the value that he attributed to it as a stimulus of good actions. If fame is rejected, what can take its place as a human motive? Without fame, "whats left to stir up humane Wit?" (st. 73). His answer is Christian virtue, a virtue that in one sense transcends the world while in another sense pro-duces action in it. Fame is "a consequence, no cause" (st. 76) of this virtue, and it will be subsumed into the larger process of an individual's holy actions as he moves through this life toward heaven. To concentrate on earthly fame is to mistake the echo for the true voice. There can be no real reward for human action but from God.

In supplying this kind of answer to the hard questions on the value of fame, Greville is assuming that his readers will respond positively to his removal of the debate from the physical world to the supernatural one. It does mark a significant shift in the terms of the discussion, and, in a sense, it allows Greville to hold on to some of the values that he attached to fame in the first half of the

poem. As Bullough observes,[10] Greville is not unlike Milton in
Lycidas who scorns fame while simultaneously acknowledging its
potency in everyday life:

> Fame is the spur that the clear spirit doth raise
> (That last infirmity of Noble mind)
> To scorn delights, and live laborious days.

Greville, as a man of the world, knows better than to imagine
that everyone will act solely out of motives of virtue. But that fact
does not mean for him that he should not continue to champion
the ideal.

IV   A Treatie of Warres

Of Wars may be dealt with rather more briefly than the other
treatises, though not necessarily because its subject is more
pedestrian. What we do not find in this poem is the practical instruction for the waging of war that was in abundance in the
twelfth section of *Monarchy*. In *Wars* Greville is concerned to a
far greater extent with the philosophical implications of war,
with what its existence says about human nature and what part it
plays in the divine plan for human affairs.

Rebholz thinks that this is the most difficult of the treatises to
date, although he suggests 1619 to 1621 as a likely possibility.[11]
Certainly there is nothing internal to the poem that points con-
clusively to any one period, but in its somberness and in the
weight of its philosophical statements it closely resembles the
manner of the final two treatises.

The poem opens with conventional praise of peace and its
blessings. War is initially presented as a perversion of the fruits of
peace. Yet war has been so common in human history that the
distinction between normality and abnormality has become confused. Again and again, rulers have acted out of the basest of
motives in leading their nations into wars that bring only suffering to their people. War cannot by attributed entirely, however,
to the malice of selfish governors, for Greville soon sets out upon a
fairly lengthy explanation of the causal relationship between sin
in all men and war. War is a mixture "of Pride, Rage, Avarice. /
Ambition, Lust, and every tragicke vice" (st. 20).[12] These
qualities are to be found in the "common staines of our Human-

ity" (st. 23), since "in our Nature . . . rebellion lives" (st. 24). Since the Fall we have become worse than devils and have brought our own hell upon us. The situation is not, however, as bleak as it might at first appear, for, as Hugh Maclean has pointed out, Greville finds that paradoxically men are often better in time of war; during a war "politicke celerity, / Diligence, courage, constancy excell" (st. 29).[13] If man can do nothing about his own corrupt nature which leads him into war, he can apparently exercise at least some limited control over his actions once that state of war is upon him.

The remainder of the poem, from stanza 31 to the end of stanza 68, turns to consider the nature of war as an instrument of God's power rather than a manifestation of man's sin. Maclean has summarized concisely the argument of this section:

Wars are sent by God for various reasons: to punish sin, to test man, to reorganize (and revivify) the social structure; notably, to maintain the process of cyclical change within the natural order. The God-directed cycle serves three ends: it simplifies and refines the "degenerations of earth" (st. 41); it purges and renews "the World" (st. 43); and, with special reference to war as symbol of "the oppositions here below," it signifies the divine promise that "Dissolution all at length must sease" (sts. 44, 48).[14]

To consider war in this light is to make of it a divine rather than a devilish thing. It would seem that Greville does, in fact, see war as possessing this dual face, and this perception aids him in accepting, perhaps even welcoming, its existence. One may despise war and its consequences on the purely human plane, but there is always available the alternative view achieved by raising the entire situation to the divine plane. Any failure to commit oneself wholly to a war, once it has started, becomes, in this view, a contravention of God's intentions. A man who, like Greville, accepts the necessity of living in a world that he despises spiritually may thus enter into a war with a clear conscience. He may pursue "Conquest, Honour, Fame" (st. 60) not because they are valuable in any absolute sense and not because these mortal achievements serve God's purpose, but rather because he is less apt to sin there than he is in several other activities and he is, in any case, making himself a soldier (albeit an ignorant one) of God as holy general.

The concluding stanza indicates the precariousness of this argument, even for its author: "Thus wave we Christians still be-

twixt two aires; / Nor leave the world for God, nor God for it"
(st. 68). The dualistic approach to existence is not a comfortable
one, and nowhere does Greville say or suggest that he has found
exactly the proper equilibrium. But he does not despair when
confronted by the challenge, and his attitude toward war
epitomizes the painful thought processes that he went through
again when trying to make sense of a human experience in which
he felt simultaneously elevated and debased.

V   A Treatie of Humane Learning

Humane Learning is, in many respects, the most interesting of
Greville's treatises for a student of literature. The treatise's concern is the life of the mind—its value, its nurture, and its
pleasures. The work thus takes its place in a group of Renaissance
discussions of the function of the intellect, the most notable of
which are Samuel Daniel's *Musophilus* (1599) and Bacon's *Advancement of Learning* (1605). Bullough thinks that Greville's
treatise was written soon after the *Advancement* appeared,[15]
while Rebholz places it considerably later, in the early 1620s,
after Greville had resumed public service but prior to the death of
King James whose ambitions toward scholarship might have been
flattered by seeing Greville's manuscript.[16]

Whoever read *Humane Learning* at whatever point in this
fifteen-year period would have found Greville's discussion of his
subject to be considerably darker in tone than had been the case
with any of the earlier contributions. While the other authors
who had taken up the subject had all, after noting several reservations, concluded that learning was a noble enterprise, Greville
seems, at least for a long while, to find little of value in the history
of man's mental activity. The traditional humanistic defense of
learning, especially of abstract learning, certainly had received a
sharp challenge from Bacon and his scoffing, pragmatic em-
piricism, but now Greville asks if *any* sort of human inquiry is
deserving of recognition. His introduction to the poem sets forth
his view of the pursuit of knowledge as merely one manifestation
of man's degeneracy; it was, after all, the principal cause of the
Fall: "This Knowledge is the same forbidden tree, / Which man
lusts after to be made his Maker" (st. 3).[17] Pursuing his skeptical
attack with increasingly greater energy, Greville faults not only
man's faculties for thought—the senses, imagination, memory,

understanding, passion, and wit—but also the fields upon which those faculties have been exercised—the sciences and the arts. If the faculties are corrupt, he asks, then what good can be expected of the final products? His supposition that even "high-prais'd Philosophie" is nothing more than "bookes of Poesie, in Prose compil'd" (st. 29) leads him steadily to the conclusion that the sum of man's wisdom is finally irrelevant to what ought to be his highest goal, the salvation of his soul.

The virtually complete skepticism that Greville displays through this section of the poem is, to some extent at least, traditional. Rosalie Colie, among others, has traced the skeptical strain of philosophy as it finds its place in Renaissance literature. She identifies Greville's skepticism as being simultaneously complete and impermanent: complete in that no one exposes the vanity of all the arts and sciences as unremittingly as he and impermanent in that his religious seriousness could not permit him to rest in and enjoy the skepticism that he had created.[18] If his spiritual well-being was beyond the influence of his efforts to learn, he nevertheless remained a functioning creature in an imperfect world, and, as such, he felt an obligation to improve that world as his talents permitted him.

He had concluded the first section of the poem by questioning in stanza 60 whether man should pay any attention at all to the pursuit of knowledge. Nothing in the poem to this point would suggest anything but a negative answer, but now, surprisingly, Greville begins a limited affirmation of the value of the intellect. His response is Baconian in its nature and shows the effects of careful reflection upon his friend's writings. Like Bacon, he is deeply distrustful of all learning that is not recognizably utilitarian, and his general prescription is that "The World should therefore her instructions draw / Backe unto life, and actions, whence they came" (st. 71). These instructions must be as direct and nontheoretical as possible: "Againe the active, necessarie Arts, / Ought to be briefe in bookes, in practise long" (st. 68).

The language in which the discourse of learning is conducted should be clear and stable, stripped of the ambiguities of theoretical philosophers and returned to the precise diction of craftsmen. All human institutions—universities, government, courts of law, medicine—must give up whatever imprecisions of concept they have acquired through the centuries in favor of simple, direct service to their constituents.

As for the "arts" by which humanity expresses and entertains
itself, they too are to be subjected to simplification and the
possibility of elimination. Grammar, logic, and rhetoric—all
mainstays of the medieval and Renaissance educational curriculum—are in advanced stages of degeneracy; they no longer
are fit instruments of communication. With Bacon, he demands a
return to clarity of expression before any meaningful communication can take place between men: "words must sparkes be of those
fires they strike" (st. 109).

When he turns to the "Arts of Recreation" (st. 111), poetry and
music, he is at first expectedly dubious about their value, noting
that they have been said to be mere entertainment and that we
cannot use them to "mend our states" (st. 111). Yet, Greville
argues, they may serve an important function after all, since
music "helps to move thoughts" when made a part of a service of
worship and since poetry can present a beautiful verbal counter-
part of divine ideals. Although poetry "seemeth onely but to
please," it in fact "teacheth us order under pleasures name" (st.
114). This didactic conception of the function of poetry shows an
indebtedness to Sidney's *Defence of Poesie*, although he by this
point in his career could not have felt, as he might once have with
Sidney, that the poet was a divine instrument of God. Now he
sees the poet as firmly mortal, as someone who can help to in-
struct through the practice of his art but who also must be careful
lest his art assume too much importance for him or for his reader.
Greville's conclusion on music and literature is that they are
"Both, ornaments to life and other Arts, / Whiles they doe serve,
and not possesse our hearts" (st. 115).

The closing section of the poem describes the relationship of the
argument that he has pursued to the group of God's "elect."
These individuals, given over to God and regenerated in the spirit
of holiness, are mentioned in all of the verse treatises. Greville
never specifies their number, but he hints in several places that if
there is to be any possibility at all for the preservation of the
world it will be because of the virtuous lives of these pure, but active, souls. In the context of the poem, they are presented as being
interested in the affairs of mortality though always aware of the
necessary subservience of the mortal to the immortal:

> Hence have they latitudes, wherein they may
> Study Sea, Skie, Ayre, Earth, as they enjoy them;
> Contemplate the Creation, State, Decay

> Of mortall things, in them that misimploy them:
> Preserve the body to obey the minde,
> Abhorre the error, yet love Humane kinde.
>
> (st. 133)

The elect know that learning should lead finally not to a sense of Baconian exaltation but rather to a feeling of profound humility. The highest knowledge is the knowledge of God, and this can be attained only through the "paine of Regeneration": "By which she [the soul] must raise herselfe againe, / Ere she can judge all other knowledge vaine" (st. 151). The desire for knowledge may be innate, Greville believes, but just as innate should be a sense of human learning's severe limitations.

VI   A Treatise of Religion

There is now general agreement that *Religion* represents the final extended literary effort that Greville made. Written in the closing years of his life, it shows clear thematic advances from the positions that he had adopted in the previous treatises. The sense of a dual commitment to the demands of heaven and the demands of earth that had so characterized the plays and the other treatises is here almost absent. In *Religion* Greville rejects the world nearly unequivocally and relinquishes whatever interest he might once have taken in its causes. The poem thus serves as a record of an arduous series of choices that have culminated in a decision that the truths of mortality are utterly inconsequential when compared with the truth of God.

Sin is, of course, one of the prevalent themes in all of Greville's work. But this poem, along with the last lyrics of *Caelica*, articulates a more overwhelming vision of the pervasiveness of sin than any other portion of his canon. The poem opens with a description of the glimmer of divinity in man that causes him to detest the sin that he has both inherited and committed and to aspire to the salvation of heaven:

> What is the chaine which drawes us backe againe,
> And lifts man up unto his first Creation?
> Nothinge in him his owne hart can restraine,
> His reason lives a captive to temptation,
>   Example is correct, precepts are mixt:
>   All fleshlie knowledge frayle, and never fixt.

It is a light, a guifte, a grace inspired,
A sparcke of power, a goodnesse of the good,
Desire in him, that never it desired,
An unitie where desolution stood;
    In us, not of us; a spirit not of earth.
    Fashioninge the mortall to immortall birth.
                                              (sts. 2–3)[19]

This self-consciousness of one's own depravity is Calvinistic in
nature, and *Religion* more than any other of his works displays
Greville's affinities with Calvin's theology. For Calvin, sinful
man was powerless to aid in his own salvation: any redemption
had to come exclusively by means of the grace of God. Some of
Greville's earlier writings, with their emphasis on the practice of
virtue in human terms as well as divine, perhaps diverged
somewhat from Calvin's position, but here he identifies himself
more clearly as a believer in heaven's sole power in these matters:

Then judge poor man! Gods Image once, 'tis true,
Though nowe the Devills, by thine owne defection,
Judge man, I say, to make this Image newe,
And clense thy fleshe from this deepe-dy'de infection,
What miracles must needes be wrought in you,
That thus stand lost in all thinges but Election?
    What livinge death, what strange illumination
    Must be inspir'd to this regeneration?

Must not the grace be supernaturall,
Which in forgivinge gives sanctification;
And from this second Chaos of his fall
Formes in mans litle world a newe Creation?
    And must not then this twice-borne child of heaven
    Bringe forth in life this newe perfection given?
                                              (sts. 41–42)

He is not, however, quite yet a thorough-going Calvinist, for as
one reads on he finds that man's response to the act of "Election"
is not what it had been for Calvin, who assumed that eternal
reward or damnation was completely predestined and that an individual could do nothing to cooperate with God in his own
salvation. But Greville wants men to know of and to acknowledge
God's gift:

Then man! pray, and obtaine; beleeve, and have;
Omnipotence and goodnesse readie be
To rayse us with our Saviour from the grave. . . .

Then till thou feele this heavenlie change in thee
Of pride, to meeknesse; Atheisme, to zeale;
Lust, unto continence; anger, to charitie;
Thou feelest of thine Election no true seale.

(sts. 43–44)

G. F. Waller has suggested that even when he had evolved to this stage of rejecting the world Greville still could not bring himself to believe that the kind of public service that men like Sidney and he had performed could go unrewarded.[20] Thus the poet argues that one not only can know that he has been regenerated by divine grace but he is also to be encouraged to continue leading a life of selfless virtue "by usinge all thinges of our owne / To others good; not to our selves alone" (st. 46). The point of leading such a godly life is not that the world might be redeemed—Greville no longer believed that anything could be done to ameliorate earthly conditions—but rather it is that such actions are the proper response of someone who wants to imitate divine goodness to the best of his frail abilities. God's will is that sin be conquered, and His strength is such that His "presence breakes sinnes middle wall in sunder" (st. 59). The elect recognize how little they can do to affect this battle, but they nevertheless must try, taking some consolation from the knowledge that they are the "Church invisible . . . fews, and good" (st. 63). For the historical "visible" church, Greville has few warm feelings. As a political body it has always been "mere hypocrisie, / The worlds Religion, borne of wit and lust" (st. 24) served by "preists of chance and gaine" (st. 68). His target is no longer mainly the Roman church and the other enemies of Anglicanism; now, it has expanded to include his own national church and any supposed manifestation of godliness that lies beyond the limits of the individual soul.

Man wants religion instinctively; of that Greville has no doubt. Our inherent sense of guilt when we see "our natures fall" into corruption will cause our souls "to finde their owner out" (st. 8) in order to try to make amends. But all historical avenues by which the soul might attain God now seem to Greville to be terribly misleading. Perhaps as God's recompense for this universal deterioration of proper homage to Him, Greville expects no further evidence of divine intervention in man's behalf:

> Arckes now wee looke for none, nor signes to part
> Egypt from Israel; all rests in the hart.
>
> (st. 95)

"All rests in the hart." With this phrase Greville defines what has come to be for him the only possible means of knowing God. The world, which had no doubt at one time seemed to him to reflect divine order, is anarchic and spiritually moribund. "Only that litle flocke, Gods owne elect, / (Who livinge in the world, yet of it are not)" (st. 111) remain to uphold the principles of faith and love. It is the testimony of a disillusioned man, of an old man. But it is also a testimony that compels respect.

CHAPTER 5

The Biographer

GREVILLE'S prose consists of his fairly extensive correspondence and two titled works, *A Letter to an Honourable Lady* and *The Life of Sir Philip Sidney*. The correspondence cannot be a major concern in this study. It has been examined, with considerable biographical profit, by Rebholz and Rees, and it is presently being edited for publication by Norman K. Farmer, Jr. The majority of the extant letters are written to Robert Cecil. They document various aspects of the life of an aspiring courtier who is reporting through them to his superior. Mundane business details, pleas for special favor, flattery, offers of gifts—so run the topics that Greville most frequently chooses to bring up with Cecil.[1] As one might expect in letters of this sort, Greville seems very careful and calculating in the presentation of himself; he rarely, if ever, gives the impression that he is setting down on paper his innermost opinions on a subject. Farmer feels that this cautiousness is not confined to the letters to Cecil, that there is a vague, almost covert quality to all of his correspondence.[2] Greville was never a man to take great risks in life, and he may have been more than usually guarded about written opinions that were certain to pass beyond his circle of friends.

Both of the titled pieces of prose are of considerably more interest to a student of Greville's poetry and thought. Both are full, discursive expositions of his attitudes, written at what were probably crucial points of transition in his philosophical development. Although neither is a striking example of literary prose in the Renaissance, both are clear, well-organized presentations of fact and argument. Their organization is perhaps in need of special emphasis, since Greville has generally been thought to be even more haphazard in his prose than in his verse treatises. How this opinion came about is something of a mystery, since attention to the progression of his analyses in the prose shows him to be at

least as much in command of his materials as Sir Thomas Browne
and almost as much as Milton. Greville can equal neither of these
later authors in the force and memorability of his style, but his
precisely delineated ideology in these tracts constitutes a significant advance in the development of Renaissance prose.

I   A Letter to an Honourable Lady

Rebholz and Rees disagree on the date of composition of the
Letter, Rebholz placing it around 1589 and Rees about a decade
later.[3] As usual, no satisfactory resolution seems possible,
although there is at least some reason to believe that there is a
more precise date for this work than for most of Greville's other
writings. That reason derives from the fact that the manuscript of
the *Letter* that lies behind the printed texts of the 1633 edition of
the *Works* and in Grosart's edition is clearly broken off and un-
finished. This lack of completeness probably indicates that
Greville did not come back to it for later tinkering, as was his
custom with his other works, and that it thus more exactly
presents his opinions at a particular time than do most of his other
pieces.

Both Rebholz and Rees agree that there is reason to suppose
that the *Letter* was written sometime in proximity to the plays,
although Rees sees it coming after the preliminary versions of
Mustapha and *Alaham* and just before the destroyed *Antony and
Cleopatra*, the thematic outline of which she supposes Greville to
present in an extended passage on Cleopatra in the *Letter*.
Rebholz's argument for a 1589 date may be thought more convincing, for he demonstrates the possible relationships between
certain of the attitudes toward human love in the *Letter* and in
the first seventy-six poems of *Caelica*, attitudes which he feels
receive quite drastic modification in all of the dramas. Certainly
it is possible to see a limited optimism about human relationships
in the *Letter* that has virtually disappeared in *Mustapha*, and an
interest in what happens in the institution of marriage that is absent from his later more exclusively political and theological
works.

The putative audience for the letter is an unnamed noble-
woman whose husband has been unfaithful to her. Whether the
letter was in fact intended for a particular woman or whether it
takes a one-woman reader as a fictional convention while actu-

ally addressing itself to a wider audience is a question as yet unresolved by available evidence. Greville's advice to the woman, real or fictive, is that she not divorce or otherwise oppose her erring husband but rather resign herself to her situation, accepting him for what he is and finding her happiness in an introspective stoic contemplation of her own virtue.

There is a larger applicability to the point of Greville's counsel here, and it is that broader point that makes the *Letter* especially interesting. In the last two of the six chapters he begins drawing explicit parallels between the lady's position in regard to her husband and the subject's in regard to his monarch. The issue thus becomes one of obedience to authority in general, and Greville's ideas on the matter here are perhaps his earliest formulation of the philosophical stoicism that was to characterize so much of his later thought. At the same time it must also be noted that here stoicism is presented in a quite positive tone as being something that can lead one to a condition of Christian joy rather than to the condition of grim pessimism that darkens the mood of his subsequent writing.

As Joan Rees has suggested, the *Letter* may indeed have served as a vehicle for Greville to work out his ideas on the story of Antony and Cleopatra. He does elaborate more on this particular example than he does on any other instance from classical and biblical history in the *Letter*. His interest in the example is in the situation of Antony's wife Octavia, a situation that he sees as analogous to that of his addressee. Octavia's behavior can be taken as a model: "dividing her innocency from his errors with the middle-wall of a severe life, she remained still his good angell."[4] Even if Rees is wrong, however, about the chronological proximity of the two works, the story of Octavia and her husband must be taken as an effective means of linking the attitudes appropriate to domesticity with those appropriate to politics, for Octavia's possible reactions to Antony's infidelity could very definitely have had national and international implications. That she "contented her sweet minde with the triumphs of patience" (282) rather than creating a public "murmur" is a decision that wins Greville's full approval.

In addition to the indirect advice of example, there is also a considerable quantity of direct admonition to the lady, counsel epitomized in the instruction that "in stead of mastering him, master your selfe" (247). She is not to

complaine or mutinie against the stronger; for the one discovers incon-
siderate weaknesse, the other languishing errors: but rather as the
vegetable things in the wisedome of Nature doe, so advise your ladyship to
doe: which is draw all your sap in this Winter of thoughts, downe to the
root; and be content to want leaves, till the sweet Spring of time or occasion come to invite them up againe. (269)

There will be temptations not to follow this course of action (or,
more accurately, of inaction), since the world would seem to offer
ample possibilities not only for redress of wrongs but for positive
enjoyment of life once errors have been set right. This apparent
gratification must, however, be seen for what it is, a sham:

Through this false Paradise—noble Lady—we must therefore passe, as
Ulysses did by the enchanted desarts of Circe; stopping our eares and closing our eyes, lest our rebellious senses, as apt to flatter as to be flattered,
chance to take part with the diversity of beguiling objects, and so lead our
misty understandings captive to perdition. . . . And in this captivity, let
no ignorance seem to excuse mankinde; since the light of truth is still neere
us, the tempter and accuser at such continuall warre within us, the lawes
that guide, so good for them that obey, and the first shape of every sinne
so ugly, as whosoever does but what he knowes, or forbeares what he
doubts, shall easily follow nature unto grace: and if he in that way obtaine not the righteousnesse of eternity, yet shall he purchase the world's
time and eternity, by morall fame. (258–59)

The pleasure that *is* possible becomes, then, an entirely inter-
nalized pleasure, but one which can nevertheless have the highest
positive consequences insofar as earthly self-discipline can lead to
the portals of divine grace. There once might have been the
possibility for personal fulfillment in the social institution of marriage, but Greville relegates that possibility to the mythic
paradise of the "Golden Age, which the allegories of the poets
figure unto us" (235). Marriage as practiced in the Golden Age,
like all other features of that era from the Renaissance perspective,[5] has now become an aspect of the past impossible to imitate
in a later "Brazen Age" that corrupts love as thoroughly as it
corrupts all other human activity. Greville's theory of history,
emphasizing as it does continual deterioration, allows him no possible hope for visible amelioration in the lady's earthly life.

The discussion of Octavia is by no means the only linking in the

Letter of private and public resignation. Indeed, as the epistle moves past its opening chapters, Greville's chief concern becomes that of the macrocosm of the body politic. At several points he notes a direct correlation between the two types of obedience:

That obedience is just, the customes of Nations and lawes of Nature will assure you; who give the mightier preeminence, and the stronger, rule. Againe, those excesses which arise out of Authority, are they not either rods of trials which we inferiors must kisse, and that God onely may burne, which made them; or else mists of mutinous self love, which deceive, and make man as well misunderstand his diseases, as their remedies? And so by misplacing equality and inequality, at once ruine both publike and private security. (279)

That such an analogue should be sought can come as no surprise, since several of the final poems in the first section of *Caelica* had clearly shown not only Greville's cynicism about the alleged pleasures of heterosexual love but also his disinclination to assign it any particular importance when compared to the concerns of government and philosophy. No matter how crucial the unnamed lady's plight might be to her, ultimately for Greville it should be subsumed into the larger issue of national rule.

It may seem curious that Greville at an early age and with as yet no particular political power of his own should retreat to such an iron-bound conservatism, a position that he was to hold in its essentials for the rest of his life, whether he was in royal favor or out. The explanation is probably to be found in part in his belief in the world's moral and physical regression. In such a state of affairs he seems to have been unwilling to risk any disruption of hierarchy that, in his view, would only speed man on his course toward chaotic individualism. To counteract this consequence of original sin, he returns constantly to the prescription of authority:

To satisfie ourselves that obedience is necessary, let us againe examine the nature of authority: and we shall finde it to bee, a commanding power, that hath relation to the obedience of inferiors. And then if we consider from what root it springeth, we shall find it to be out of nature in some things, in others from a lavish giving away of our owne liberties. . . . Out of which particulars I thinke we may conclude obedience to be necessary; and that they who strive to remove the unremoveable rockes with chaines, draw themselves to the rockes, but not the rockes to them. Neither in this question is the difference between supreme or meane authority materiall, nor what diverse foundations they have; since it falls out in Power as it doth in Knowledge; that who is any thing at all is all the world above us. (277–78)

If this prescription conforms, as Greville insists that it does, to the laws of nature, it also enables the obedient wife/subject to polish her spiritual attributes preparatory to eternity. Rebholz feels that this indicates a belief on Greville's part at this time in the close and compatible relationship between the realms of nature and grace.[6] Certainly there is nothing in the *Letter* to deny this hypothesis and a fair amount of evidence to support it. As A. S. P. Woodhouse demonstrated many years ago with reference to Spenser and Milton, men of the Renaissance were accustomed to thinking of the separateness of, as well as the interaction between, the physical and spiritual in man's life,[7] and Greville too seems interested in conceptualizing of human existence in this frame of reference. He urges the lady to believe that even if she should lose both her husband and the world she might still

winne credit with God. In which mysticall worke the fine mixture of grace and nature stand together, makes it more easie to mend our errours, than before it was to cover them; and consequently our flesh as capable to receive the immortality of good, as it was to run headlong under the eternall curse of the sinne. (291)

In view of the skepticism about man's capacity to affect his own spiritual condition that Greville was to adopt later in life, the fact that he here finds it "easie" to mend "errours," both spiritual and physical, is worthy of special notice. One suspects that he soon came to see his statement as no more than mere words.

II The Life of Sir Philip Sidney

Although Greville's friendship with Philip Sidney constituted one of his principal poles of emotional and moral inspiration, his inability to memorialize in an adequate way Sidney's short life seems also to have been a continuing source of frustration for him. The forty-two years separating the two men's deaths were for Greville a period of prolonged mourning, gratitude, and irritation. His pleasure at having known Sidney closely was tempered frequently by his sense of distress over his nation's failure to uphold the principles that he felt Sidney had represented.

The fact that Greville was sufficiently proud of his relationship with Sidney to include "Friend to Sir Philip Sidney" in the inscription on his tomb along with his statement of service to two monarchs is indicative of what he felt Sidney meant to him and to England. In Sidney, Greville saw a model of perfection of both the private and the public man, the private individual whose ordered, pious life had been put into the public service of humanistic learning and a reformed Christian England.

Frequently in Sidney's company while both were alive, Greville also walked next to Sidney's body in the funeral procession that was the expression of a nation's grief in 1586. He was doubtless thrown into a state of considerable psychological depression by the death, and the next few years were probably ones of relative literary inactivity. With the possible exceptions of a few lyrics that eventually took their places in *Caelica* and of the *Letter to an Honourable Lady*, probably written in 1589, Greville's literary energies during this period were directed toward the preparation of an edition of selected works of Sidney. Within a month of Sidney's death, Greville wrote to his friend's father-in-law, Sir Francis Walsingham, to pass along to him a rumor he had heard that there was soon to appear a pirated edition of the first version of the *Arcadia*, assuring Walsingham that he would do whatever he could to make "a stay of that mercenary book" and prevent Sidney's honor from being besmirched by the publication of the unrevised manuscript.[8] Having succeeded, at least for the time being, at stopping an unauthorized edition, he undertook an edition of his own, basing it on the revised manuscript which Sidney had left with him. It is clear from what he says in the *Life* that his preference in Sidney's canon was for his friend's more overtly religious translations, but, since nothing that Sidney had written was in his view impious or unhelpful to a confused sinner, he was no doubt satisfied to help bring into the world the 1590 quarto edition of the first two books of the *Arcadia* and a portion of the third.

Twenty years passed before Greville probably began work on the *Life*. As is the case with several of his other productions, it exists in more than one version—in four, to be exact. Rebholz and Rees agree that most, if not all, of the versions can be placed in the decade of Greville's forced retirement, from 1604 to 1614, with 1610 as the most likely date for the beginning of his work on the project.[9] At about the same time he was planning to write a life of Elizabeth, a biography which, like that of Sidney, would have served to illustrate how far the nation had fallen from its days of past grandeur. But Cecil denied him access to the governmental papers that he would have needed for the book, a rebuff that probably accounts for the presence of an elaborate digression on Elizabeth's reign in the revised versions of the *Life of Sidney*. Unable to write the complete history that he wanted to do, Greville seems to have decided to combine his two projects since the didactic ends of both were similar. A recent study by Mark L. Caldwell has traced some of the sources that Greville may have used for the political history in the *Life* and has shown this history to be a complementary expansion of the portrait of Sidney that Greville presents elsewhere in the work.[10] Virtue in the microcosm of the man becomes, in this view, most interesting and most valuable, when it can be shown to have larger manifestations in the macrocosm of the world.

A *Purpose*

To mention the political content of the *Life* is to involve oneself in an estimation of Greville's intentions in composing the piece. Politics do figure highly in the plan of the *Life*, and one may reasonably suppose that Greville saw his presentation of what was to him the commendable political condition of Elizabeth's reign as another version of the thinly veiled criticism of James' rule that was present in the plays. Sidney's short career as a courtier naturally lent itself to a discussion of the political life of his era, but Greville accentuates this natural tendency with two lengthy sections that have only a tenuous connection to a narrative of Sidney's life: the so-called "Map of Europe," a survey of international relations in the 1580s (chapters 8–10 of Smith's 1907 edition) and the description of Elizabeth's governance of her realm (chapters 15–17). These features, which will be considered in greater detail a bit later, contribute markedly to the political tone of the *Life*.

Probably of greater interest to the modern reader, however, are those parts of the work that deal most directly with Sidney as a man and as a poet. There is little objectivity in these passages, and it quickly becomes clear to the reader that what Greville is presenting here is an evolution of the genre of the saint's life:

For my own part, I observed, honoured, and loved him so much; as with what caution soever I have passed through my dayes hitherto among the living, yet in him I challenge a kind of freedome even among the dead. So that although with Socrates, I professe to know nothing for the present; yet with Nestor I am delighted in repeating old newes of the ages past; and will therefore stir up my drooping memory touching this mans worth, powers, wayes, and designes: to the end that in the tribute I owe him, our nation may see a Sea-mark, rais'd upon their native coast, above the levell of any private Pharos abroad: and so by a right Meridian line of their own, learn to sayl through the straits of true vertue, into a calm, and spacious Ocean of humane honour. (3)[11]

Greville's devotion to this hagiographic end is unflagging. Whatever twists and turns his narrative might take, he never sounds a note on Sidney himself save those of enthusiastic praise. The exemplum of Sidney's life is clearly intended, as suggested in this passage, to serve as a standard of Christian virtue for all those lesser spirits in need of a sense of moral direction.

A third goal for Greville is the exposition of Sidney's system of aesthetics, especially for purposes of contrasting them with Greville's own. In fact, Greville's views on literature diverged rather sharply from Sidney's, although he chooses here to subordinate those differences, principally by distorting somewhat the nature of Sidney's literary achievement while taking the opportunity to argue for a theory of literature that Sidney would probably not have embraced.

Given these ends, it should be quite clear that one thing that the *Life* is *not* is a biography in the modern sense of the word, although it has sometimes been supposed to be such and has then been judged a failure from the standpoint of objectivity and technique. The title of the book, *The Life of the Renowned Sir Philip Sidney*, naturally arouses expectations of biography, but the title is not Greville's but rather that of the publisher who first printed the book in 1652. In his opening paragraph Greville gives the reader a more accurate description of his own conception of the work, calling it a "dedication" to the memory of Sidney and indicating that its function is to serve as a preface to a volume of *Alaham, Mustapha*, and an early version of *A Treatise of Monarchy*, all works which he offhandedly relegates to the category of "exercises of my youth." One may suppose that this denigration is, to some extent at least, *pro forma* since Greville, even though coming to see all mortal efforts as vanity, would hardly attempt to memorialize Sidney with a volume of literature in which he could take no pride. What caused him to change his mind and not carry through with his plans for the publication of his manuscript will probably never be clear.

This various mixture of fact, preaching, and literary criticism does not, however, render the *Life* devoid of biographical value. In it are to be found, among other things, some of the famous anecdotes that did much to shape the popular image of Sidney, both in his own era and in ours. The well-known quarrel with the earl of Oxford on the royal tennis courts, a quarrel in which the young Sidney coolly stood his ground with the peer after having been called a "puppy," is here as is the classic example of Renaissance gallantry, Sidney's insistence on the battlefield at Zutpen that a wounded foot soldier drink water before he would drink of it even though he was mortally wounded himself.

These vignettes, and others like them, cannot help but be interesting to the reader. If the *Life* were composed of such a series of anecdotes and reminiscences, it could easily be categorized and accepted for what it was. But the problem, from the standpoint of modern biography, is that Greville does not content himself with this sort of effort. Rather, as has been shown, the *Life* sets itself several ambitious goals, but the models of biography available to Greville and his own limitations as a writer of narrative prevent his fulfilling these goals in an aesthetically pleasing way. The *Life* is marred by a lack of control in conception and structure, with the consequence that a certain formlessness becomes one of its most noticeable characteristics. As one reads through it, one has to labor at several points to recall just where Greville seemed to be headed prior to beginning whatever digression he is currently involved in. Still, as Caldwell has observed, if the two largest digressions—the "Map of Europe" in chapters 8–10 and the history of Queen Elizabeth in chapters 15–17—are set aside, one is left with a more straightforward memoir of Sidney's youth and brief adulthood than one might at first suppose to be the case.[12] Lacking the tightness and the sense of priorities of a modern biography, Greville's *Life* nevertheless does proceed in a generally chronological fashion and does have, as the following discussion will show, a sense of shape, if not in minutiae then in the overall pattern.

B   *Political Content*

Of the three kinds of exposition—political, moral, and aesthetic—in the *Life*, the political is perhaps most easily grasped. The more that is known of the circumstances surrounding the composition of the *Life*, the more apparent the political elements of the work become. There can be little doubt that during the years following Elizabeth's death in 1603, Greville came to develop a distinct preference for the days of her reign when he compared them to the policies and personalities of the court of James. The effects of this attitude on his other writings—on the dramas and on *Caelica*—are inspected elsewhere in this study, and now it will suffice to mention what Greville may have seen as a distillation of that contrast in the characters of Sidney and Robert Cecil, earl of Salisbury. It was, of course, true that James could not be held entirely responsible for the policies of Cecil; Elizabeth had, after all, made him her secretary of state and had chosen him as her nearly sole confidant during her final months. But after having successfully made the transition between monarchs, Cecil continued to exert considerable influence over the new king. Unfortunately for Greville, Cecil seems always to have been rather distrustful of him and now, under the new monarch, Cecil opened a fissure between the two men that was to grow steadily wider. Kept from the court until Cecil's death in 1612, Greville had ample time and inclination to cultivate his dislike of Cecil and what he stood for. Cecil's forbidding of Greville to have access to the state council papers when Greville wanted to do his more extensive history of Elizabeth's reign no doubt had the effect of deepening Greville's bitterness and of helping him decide to insert the relatively brief panegyric of the Elizabethan era in the *Life* to give that work a sharper political point.

Caldwell has written the fullest evaluation of the politics of the *Life*, showing Greville's indebtedness to William Camden's *Annales Rerum Anglicarum et Hibernicarum Regnante Elizabetha*. Although this long Latin work did not appear in print until 1615, and then only the part covering Elizabeth's reign down to 1588, Greville, as one of Camden's chief patrons, could easily have con-

sulted his protégé's work in manuscript. Caldwell has shown his
borrowings from Camden's text to be intermittent and rather ran-
dom, with "no sign of a systematic attempt to telescope the whole
Annales, or to reproduce fully a small part of it."[13] The depen-
dence upon Camden and other historians such as John Foxe and
Thomas Overbury is more notable in the sections of the *Life* given
over to matter other than that which pertains directly to Sidney.
Chapters 8–10 and 15–17 are thus simultaneously the most dense-
ly factual and the least personal portions of the book.

The tribute to Elizabeth that constitutes the second of these
two sections is not so much developed by means of noncontextual
praise of her genius as it is by frequent comparisons of her techniques of ruling with those of her successor James. The king is
never explicitly named in these contrasts, and certainly the
criticisms could be directed at any erring head of state, but the
point is always clear: "Againe in the latitudes which some
moderne Princes allow to their Favorites, as supporters of
Government, and middle wals between power, and the people's
envy; it seems this Queen reservedly kept entrenched within her
native strengths, and Scepter"(176). Even Essex, Greville goes on
to say, was never given the kind of responsibility that would
"change the tenure of commanding power, into a kind of un-
princely mediation." A strong monarch, as the dramas and verse
treatises emphasize, does not need to worry excessively about the
machinations of underlings, because those machinations operate
with little or no effectual force behind them. Not only favorites
but also clergy, parliaments, and state councils were, in Greville's
word, "used" by Elizabeth for the achieving of governmental
ends. A typical council meeting found her listening with "respect"
to divergent opinions from her ministers, then making "a quin-
tessence of all their concords, or discords within her selfe, from
whence the resolutions and directions came suddenly, and secretly
forth for execution" (188–89). This capacity for decision making
instilled a sense of "awe" in her subordinates, an awe which became "her antidote against any farther necessity of punishments."
Thus in the "arts of men, and Government, her nature, education, and long experience . . . made her become excellent above
both Sexes" (189).

Caldwell thinks that he has found analogues to the survey of
European politics in chapter 8—by far the less interesting of the
two digressions—in contemporary "intelligencers" or reports on

foreign affairs such as Butter's *New Survey of the Affaires of Europe* (1623) and Overbury's *Observations in his Travailes upon the State of the XVII Provinces as they Stood Anno Dom. 1609* (1626). Although Greville could not have seen these first printed instances of the genre from the 1620s, Caldwell assumes a familiarity on his part with the manuscript intelligencers produced in the sixteenth century.[14] Whereas this part of Caldwell's interpretation may be thought less convincing than his discovery of Camden as a source, it is possible that Greville was indeed following the pattern of such surveys. In any case, he obviously feels it desirable to show Sidney's (and his own) familiarity with contemporary political events. If one is not stirred by knowledge of how matters stood in the Hanseatic League in the 1580s, it is nevertheless possible that Greville thought that a seventeenth-century audience might profit from a review of recent history and from knowing Sidney's opinions on that history.

C   *The* Life *as Moral Tract*

Instructive though he found the political point of the *Life* to be, Greville also saw its value as a conveyer of personal morals to be significantly more important. What Joan Rees calls the "moral allegory" of the *Life* is never far from Greville's consciousness.[15] Sidney's life was in his eyes a series of events that had meaning extending far beyond their particular sets of circumstances. Rees thinks that this explains the principle of selection that Greville used for the inclusion of detail in the narrative. Personal detail is never mentioned if it might seem to exist only for its own sake;[16] thus the presence of Lady Sidney at her husband's deathbed goes unreported, since it apparently did not serve for Greville as the kind of biographical symbol that could be expanded in the reader's mind into a pattern for living. When he praises Sidney's talent in the *Arcadia* for turning "barren Philosophy precepts into pregnant Images of Life" (15), Greville is also commenting on his own goals in his biography.

Throughout the narrative, Sidney is always represented as an exemplar of conduct. Even his childhood is spoken of in terms that emphasize his mature sagacity. Greville says that he "never knew him other than a man: with such staiednesse of mind, lovely, and familiar gravity, as carried grace, and reverence above greater years"(6). This rather forbidding and Jesus-like

precociousness becomes perfectly consistent with the portrait that
Greville limns in the rest of the work, emphasizing again and
again the importance of a firm and rather somber religion as a
motivating and organizing force for Sidney's prodigious talents:
"Above all, he made the Religion he professed, the firm Basis of
his life: For this was his judgment (as he often told me) that our
true-heartedness to the Reformed Religion in the beginning,
brought Peace, Safetie, and Freedome to us" (35). Sidney's
radical protestantism provides at least an ostensible reason for all
of the political actions that Greville describes. His desire would
seem to be that of making Sidney into as dynamic a Christian
prince as possible, although it must also be noted that he does not
elect to present him as a purely active, political individual. The
classic Christian dichotomy of action and passion is present here,
at least in the depiction of Sidney's final days where Greville
speaks of him as "one to whom a stronger Spirit had given power
above himself, either to do, or suffer" (131).

One fact working against Greville's version of Sidney as a national moral leader is the brevity of Sidney's life. Advantageous in
some respects, suggesting as it does a martyr's early death,
Sidney's short existence nevertheless did not give Greville a particularly large supply of materials for hagiography. That Sidney
was a talented young government servant on whom Elizabeth
particularly cast her eye no one would deny. That he managed to
accomplish important attainments in diplomatic, military, and
philosophical matters prior to his death is a far more dubious
proposition. Thus, Greville finds himself in the position of being
forced to extrapolate on several occasions from what Sidney actually accomplished to what he might have been able to do if
longer life had been given to him. For example, the issue of
Sidney's lack of any particular political office is dismissed as unimportant: "And although he never was Magistrate, nor possessed
of any fit stage for eminence to act upon, . . . [yet] I may well
say that this Gentlemans large, yet uniform disposition was every
where praised; greater in himself than in the world; yet greater
there in fame and honour than many of his superiors"(38–39).
Greville's insistence on these points is not especially hyperbolic;
large numbers of Englishmen *did* recognize Sidney's intrinsic
worth. Few, however, would have been as absolutely certain on
the topic as is Greville.

The centrality of Sidney's radical protestantism to the analysis

of his decisions, of his actions, of all his ethical judgments affords
Greville the opportunity for yet another series of contrasts between the values of Sidney's era and those of Greville's own age.
The contrasts are not exclusively political in this case, and, for
that matter, there is not always a clear preference for the
Elizabethan period over the Jacobean. If the men of earlier
decades were superior to those of 1610, it is not necessarily because they were inherently better than their sons but rather
because of their fortunate proximity to the examples of Sidney
and Elizabeth. Indeed, at one point, Greville places even the
Elizabethan era into the Christian pessimist's view of the
deterioration of the universe: "With which solid, and active
reaches of his [Sidney's], I am perswaded, he would have found,
or made a way through all the traverses, even of the most weak
and irregular times. But it pleased God in this decrepit age of the
world, not to restore the image of her ancient vigour in him,
otherwise than as in a lightning before death" (36–37). Sidney's
own Christian humanism had probably given him a more benign
view of his epoch; he was far more convinced than the Greville of
1611 of the efficacy of purposeful human action and of the poten-
tiality for improvement in man's nature. It is dubious that he had
shared Greville's belief (derived ultimately from Augustine) that
the chronologically primitive ages were also the most perfect.
Sidney's views are, however, relatively unimportant in passages
such as this one which comment far more extensively on Greville
than they do on Sidney. Greville's conviction of the progressive
decline of society is both implicit and explicit through the *Life*,
and the pessimistic view of Jacobean England, from this point of
view, thus becomes something that is to a considerable extent inevitable. Greville still is doubtless bitter about James' failure to
recognize and properly reward his talents, and his preference for
Elizabeth can still be expressed in relatively personal terms, but
the larger moral pattern of history as he reads it shows him that
Sidney's existence was something of a temporary fluke, a momen-
tary reprieve from the steadily worsening paralysis of the human
condition.

Although England had been lucky to enjoy Sidney's presence
when it did, his life nevertheless owed something to its immediate
context as well as to God's will. Sidney's parents are presented as
precisely the right kind of moral benefactors to their first-born
child, with the "clearnesse of his Fathers judgment" and his

mother's "ingenious sensiblenesse" combining in him to form "the
extension of their strength, and the very acme, and perfect type of
it" (5-6). The Sidney family represents for Greville the highest
variety of nobility that England can hope to enjoy, but he, like
Spenser, does not suppose an automatic connection between good
birth and virtue. In the preface to book 6 of *The Faerie Queene*,
Spenser had made it clear that true "Princely curtesie" was appropriate to a person of noble blood, but while it could be expected often to be found there, there was no necessary correlation
since a nobleman could sometimes conduct himself basely. Just
so, Greville is careful to point out that any praise of Sidney must
ultimately be directed to his personal strength rather than to that
of his family; they can only help, "for the greatness which he af-
fected was built upon true Worth; esteeming Fame more than
Riches, and Noble actions far above Nobility it self" (38).

There is a democratizing effect to this sort of proposition, placing, as it does, the virtues of nobility apparently within the reach
of all. It is dubious that the politically conservative Greville
would have wanted to extend his point that far; he was genuinely
impressed with the quality of Sidney's lineage. At the same time,
however, he saw no reason to use social rank as a limiting force in
the appreciation and emulation of Sidney's life. In a passage at
the beginning of the *Life*, Greville had said that he wanted
Sidney's example to serve as a "Sea-mark" for "our nation"(3).
Much later, in the chapter describing Sidney's death, he speaks of
his friend's passage through the world as "a short progress to a
long home, passing fair, and wel-drawn lines; by the guide of
which, all pilgrims of this life may conduct themselves humbly
into the haven of everlasting rest"(127–28). That Greville insists
on this universal applicability of Sidney and of his own biography
in an age that he finds to be degenerate is one of his final appeals
to men to come to their senses and perhaps his last concession to
the notion that literature can in fact persuade.

D *The* Life *and the Art of Poetry*

In Greville's eyes Sidney epitomized the concept of balanced
virtuosity to which we have come to give the title of "Renaissance
gentleman." The *Life* attempts to portray Sidney as a "true
modell of Worth; A man fit for Conquest, Plantation, Reforma-
tion, or what Action soever is greatest, and hardest amongst men"

(33). Notable by its absence from this particular list is the achievement for which we most remember Sidney—his accomplishments as an imaginative writer. It is not a question of Greville's not having a sufficient interest in Sidney as an author. Indeed, the *Life* contains important discussions of Sidney's literary achievement. It is true, however, that Greville seems to have quite ambivalent attitudes toward Sidney's position as a writer and that he certainly would not want to include a literary career in the list of far more active vocations that he views as fit outlets for Sidney's talents. Sidney himself would probably not have placed a particularly high priority on his efforts as an author, even though it is certain that he had a more appreciative estimate of literature than did Greville in 1611. The net result of this difference in perspective between the two men is that Greville somewhat distorts Sidney's beliefs about literature, attempting to draw Sidney away from a belief in the intrinsic value of literature and toward his own position that held literature to be defensible only to the extent that it was able to produce objectively ascertainable moral responses in its readers.

Greville's own edition of the *Arcadia* in 1590 might be taken as some indication of his views on Sidney's writing, although chance may have played a role here too. The 1590 quarto is essentially the revised or "new" *Arcadia* to the point that Sidney had completed this second version in book 3. We do not know to what extent Greville had access to the manuscript of the "old" *Arcadia*, which presumably was in the possession of the countess of Pembroke, as he prepared his edition. It is highly probable, however, that even if he had had equal contact with both texts he would have chosen to publish the *New Arcadia* since, as critics unanimously agree, Sidney's revision is a far more serious, dignified, and far less frivolous work of literature than is the *Old Arcadia*. While, for example, the *Old Arcadia* had had relatively little in the way of political content, the *New Arcadia* contains a good deal on politics, or, as Greville chooses to summarize it at one point: "the growth, state, and declination of Princes, change of Government, and lawes: visissitudes of sedition, faction, succession, confederacies, plantations, with all other errors, or alterations in publique affaires" (15). As Amphialus, Basilius, Euarchus, and Sidney's other political characters deal with these matters, Greville contemplates the results much as though he was commenting on an actual series of political developments in

106   FULKE GREVILLE

English government(13–17). This deliberate breaking down of
the barrier between fiction and fact proves useful to Greville's
concept of Sidney in the *Life* as a whole since, as Rees observes, it
affords Greville the opportunity of presenting Sidney as governor,
albeit an imaginary one, manipulating men in a community so as
best to make use of their various strengths.[17] The implication that
Greville wishes to convey is clearly that Sidney the national
leader would have had no more difficulty controlling "alterations
in publique affaires" than does Sidney the author.

In the aforementioned letter to Sidney's father-in-law Sir Francis Walsingham, Greville cited, besides the *Arcadia*, Sidney's
translations of the work of the French protestant, du Plessis Mor-
nay, of the religious verse of Du Bartas, and of the Psalms. It is
curious that he does not choose to mention these translations in
the *Life*, since they could only have added to the pious luster of
Sidney's image. What is not so surprising is his omission of any
reference to Sidney's secular verse, especially to *Astrophil and
Stella*. To have given any attention to that would have been to
admit that Sidney devoted some of his energy to literature that
Greville by this point considered of far less value, and that is an
admission that Greville seems determined not to make. In fact,
interested though he is at what Sidney as the man of letters wrote,
Greville indicates at one point his approval of Sidney's supposed
deathbed disavowal of his literature: "when his body declined,
and his piercing inward powers were lifted up to a purer Horizon,
he then discovered, not onely the imperfection, but vanitie of
these shadowes, how daintily soever limned: as seeing that even
beauty it self, in all earthly complexions, was more apt to allure
men to evill, than to fashion any goodness in them"(16). It is difficult to suppose that Greville really thought that the world
would have been better off had Sidney never written a line, but
this is a logical (if extreme and impassioned) conclusion to the
kind of morality he attributed to Sidney and to the priorities that
he argued were present in Sidney's life.

Greville's biography of Sidney is, of course, itself a piece of
literature, despite his apparent conviction that it exists solely for
didactic ends. It may, however, have been forgotten by this point
that the ostensible immediate cause for the composition of the
Life was to serve as a memorial preface to a selected edition of
Greville's own works. He had mentioned this on the first page of
the *Life*, but he does not return to the subject of his personal

career as an author until the final two chapters where he moves from the history of Elizabeth's reign to his own part in that history to his writings. The passage is of significance for what it says about Greville's literary principles and how they contrast with Sidney's. He compares the two men's artistic productions in one of the most well-known passages in the *Life*:

For my own part, I found my creeping Genius more fixed upon the Images of Life, than the Images of Wit, and therefore chose not to write to them on whose foot the black Oxe had not already trod, as the Proverbe is, but to those only, that are weather-beaten in the Sea of this World, such as having lost the sight of their Gardens, and groves, study to saile on a right course among Rocks, and quick-sands; . . . thus ordaining, and ordering matter, and forme together for the use of life . . . (224)

The relevance of the statement to his own poetry will be taken up in the following chapter, just as what he goes on to say about the internalization of his dramas in the mind of the reader has been discussed in the chapter on the plays. At present it will suffice to note that he concludes the *Life* on a note of artistic and biographical honesty. Sidney *was* a different sort of writer from him, he admits, and he cannot suppose otherwise. There had been a witty beauty to Sidney's works that he now acknowledges was perhaps not immediately applicable to life, especially to life in a steadily falling world.

Ultimately, this progressive deterioration of mankind has made Sidney's achievement into something of an archaism for Greville. He concludes the biography hoping that no one will try to imitate Sidney's sort of literature:

So that howsoever I liked them [Sidney's works] too well (even in that unperfected shape they were) to condescend that such delicate (though inferior) Pictures of himselfe, should be suppressed; yet I do wish that work may be the last in this kind, presuming no man that followes can ever reach, much less go beyond that excellent intended patterne of his. (223–24)

To attempt to copy Sidney now would be pointless since his literary "delicacy" would be wasted on an age of brass. Now, the most that could be expected from literature was immediate practical guidance of the sort that he saw embodied in his own works. Or did he? It must be remembered, after all, that Greville published neither the *Life* nor his own plays and treatises while he was alive. Why he backed away from publication, after everything had been written, is not completely clear. It may be that he was, in fact, proceeding with publication plans in 1612 when Cecil died and he saw the way cleared for his return to government, a way that might well have been impeded by having his views in the *Life* and the plays achieve currency. There can be no certainty that this was the case, however, and it may equally well be that he soon despaired of the efficacy of publishing even his own works during his lifetime, preferring perhaps to let his literary survivors do with them what he had done with Sidney's texts and turn them into a posthumous memorial to him if they so desired. Milton's speaker pays public tribute to Lycidas while simultaneously hoping that some future poet will "with lucky words favor my destined urn." A far more pessimistic Greville cannot bring himself to praise his dearest friend publicly, and he could have had but little hope that anyone would ever so honor him. The irony of his works' eventual publication, and of praise for them, would have struck even his most ironic temperament as unexpected.

CHAPTER 6

The Religious Poet

IT should be obvious by this point that Greville's poetic achievement is uneven in its nature. Nowhere is this unevenness more apparent than in the lyrics that make up the final section of *Caelica*. The twenty-six poems from sonnet 84 through sonnet 109 include a half-dozen of his best-known works. The tendency in discussions of this section of the cycle has been to ignore those lyrics that do not measure up to the standard set by the finest poems and to assume a unity of theme and accomplishment that in fact does not exist. The present discussion of the conclusion of the cycle will probably not correct this tendency; it is natural to want to examine a poet's best poems and somewhat perverse to give equal treatment to his lesser moments. But the situation must be mentioned at the outset as a means of indicating that Greville's mature lyrics are not all of a piece and that any attempt to make them seem so distorts the nature of *Caelica*.

The earlier discussion of the love (or "antilove") poems in the sonnet cycle set out the variety of subjects Greville chose to pursue in that section and the number of forms in which those subjects found expression. If the range of themes and forms is somewhat narrower at the end of the cycle, it nevertheless is sufficiently broad to make fast generalizations about it impossible. The poems do turn away from love, although reference to this passion reappears from time to time, usually as something to be contrasted with concerns that Greville holds to be more important. Also, the poems turn toward religion, although spiritual matters are placed in a secular context often enough to make one aware of the persistence of politics as a vital concern to Greville until near the very end of his life. The poems that I have already suggested as being Greville's "best" are those that are most obviously and personally religious. That this is so doubtless says something about our age's belief that a lyric is most successful when it is most private, an opinion not necessarily shared by all Elizabethans.

While it is now generally thought that Greville wrote the poems in this section of *Caelica* after 1604, with the majority of them set down before his return to public life in 1614 and the last few awaiting his final years, there once again can be no exact dates attached to them.[1] If it can be assumed that the poems are to at least some extent autobiographical, if the penitence and the sense of spiritual renewal that some of them describe is Greville's own, then they must have been composed in the final phase of his career, most of them after he had written the *Life of Sidney* in 1610. I think that such an assumption can be made, since if ever autobiographical interpretations of poetry were justifiable, these poems, with their straightforward intensity, justify it. One never feels in reading them that Greville is developing a narrative personality that will intrude itself between the reader and the theme, as is frequently the case with Donne's religious lyrics, but rather one can only notice (or perhaps fail to notice) that personality is here firmly subjugated to the cause of directness of expression. There need be no insistence on autobiography in reading the lyrics, and, indeed, the discussion that follows will pay very little attention to the subject. Let it suffice now to note that the mature Greville could hardly have agreed with Sidney that the poet creates a world that never existed, a world filled with things "better than Nature bringeth forth." Greville's world is always profoundly real, always filled with the deficiencies of human existence as he observed them.

The cataloging and analysis of man's errors that he undertakes has, in the majority of instances, a centripetal energy behind it as he focuses his examination on his own failings. Various biographical circumstances no doubt combined to lead him to these repeated moments of introspection: his dissatisfaction with his part in his nation's political life, his continuing inability to ameliorate the pain caused by the death of Sidney, his failure to secure any satisfactory love with a woman, and his ever-increasing commitment to a severe and rigorous protestantism. Given these situations, it is reasonable to suppose that several of the more personal lyrics—the well-known sonnets 98 and 99, for instance—were composed as types of spiritual exercises to facilitate concentration on personal repentance and unmerited redemption. There does not seem to have been any conscious at-

tempt on Greville's part to model these poems on the structure of
formal religious meditations, as Louis Martz has shown to have
been the case with other seventeenth-century poets such as Donne
and Crashaw,[2] but Greville does nevertheless dissect his own
emotions with every bit as much precision and rigor as would
someone following such a manual of spiritual discipline.

Since there is little reason to doubt that these lyrics were not
written in chronological order, this discussion of them will progress numerically, with one exception. The poems often fall into
clusters that treat varieties of a common theme, although there
are also several poems that stand more or less alone, apparent
anomalies of thought in the loose pattern of the cycle. Some of
these can be connected to ideas that Greville worked out more
fully in one or more of the treatises. One such example is sonnet
91, and it is with this poem that I will begin, nonchronologically:

> Rewards of earth, Nobilitie and Fame,
> To senses Glorie, and to conscience woe,
> How little be you, for so great a name?
> Yet lesse is he with men that thinks you so.
>   For earthly Power, that stands by fleshly wit,
>   Hath banish'd that Truth, which should governe it.
>
> Nobilitie, Powers golden fetter is,
> Wherewith wise Kings subjection doe adorne,
> To make men thinke her heavy yoke, a blisse.
> Because it makes him more than he was borne.
>   Yet still a slave, dimm'd by mists of a Crowne,
>   Lest he should see, what riseth, what puls downe.
>
> Fame, that is but good words of evill deeds,
> Begotten by the harme we have, or doe,
> Greatest farre off, least ever where it breeds,
> We both with dangers and disquiet wooe.
>   And in our flesh (the vanities false glasse)
>   We thus deceav'd adore these Calves of brasse.[3]

The poem has quite obvious affinities with *An Inquisition upon
Fame and Honour*, not the least of which is the stanzaic form. (It
might be noted in passing that this six-line stanza is the exclusive
form in fifteen of the poems in this last section, being used in the
more private and more public lyrics alike.) But these three stanzas
are quite different in nature than any comparable fragment of the

longer poem because of their self-contained intimacy. By apos-
trophizing nobility and fame in the poem's opening line, Greville
makes of the poem a personal utterance; the judgments that
follow will be the judgments of an individual, albeit one whose
tone suggests that his opinion is that of a community of right-
thinking men. The cynicism of the final couplet in the first stanza
is the cynicism of someone who, like Greville, finds his services
unwanted by rulers who, he feels, should be able to value his
talents more accurately. The other two stanzas go on to supply
definitions that point up the weaknesses of both nobility and
fame. Titles of nobility, which other men seem to strive for as
prizes, are in Greville's view merely methods of requiring alle-
giance where none is perhaps merited and of thus fending off
potential rivals. As for fame, the more closely one inspects it, the
more quickly it evaporates. The rejection of both attributes is as
strong here as in any of the treatises. The closing allusion to the
idolatry condemned by Moses makes nobility and fame not only
frivolous but also ungodly. The poem thus serves as a general
warning against infatuation with these temptations as well as a
personal effort on Greville's part to renounce two goals toward
which he had directed much of his career.

If this poem seems to be spoken in a voice that is half-public,
half-private, the majority of the other poems discussed in this
chapter tend more toward the direction of privacy. The poem
that opens this section, sonnet 84, is highly personal in its applicability to the thematic development of the entire cycle, while at
the same time it remains accessible to anyone interested in
Greville's major emphases. The sonnet serves as a farewell to
earthly love—an attitude that earlier sonneteers, notably Wyatt
and Sidney, had already used as the genesis of some of their most
memorable poems. The placement of the sonnet is, as Gary Litt has
noted, crucial to any sense of unifying architectonics in the sequence as a whole.[4] Appearing at the end of the sonnets given over
to analysis of mundane preoccupations, this poem signals the end
of human love as a vital force in Greville's poetic consciousness.

The ruefulness that distinguishes the tone of the poem is
established in several ways. There is little in the way of outright
resentment on Greville's part for having been deceived into
wasting his time and life on love. Rather, there is an acknowl-
edgement that he freely chose to dally while other men were
working. The only partially ironic deference that he still pays to

Cupid ("Yong Master") reveals a man who can still see the attractiveness of "wanton Visions." To the extent that such an attitude condemns, it directs its condemnation not at love, which is presented as being childishly and coquettishly innocent, but rather at the mature man who ought to have known better but who could not resist. The final couplet continues and brings to a climax the irony of the preceding twelve lines. Rather than slamming the door on all frivolity, Greville's decision to "play me" with higher, less pleasing thoughts leaves it open a crack, at least for nostalgic backward glances at that which he once permitted himself to enjoy. And when he does mention love in subseuent poems, while it consistently receives brusque treatment, it is never more severely condemned than any other mortal enterprise.

Sonnet 85 is clearly a companion piece for sonnet 84. A detailed description of heavenly love, it presents Greville's new goal for both his life and his poetry. While other sonnet cycles might have ended with sonnet 84, *Caelica* turns now to approach other themes. This fact can, of course, be used to argue either for or against any concept of unifying structure in the cycle, although I would prefer to think that Greville uses this transition to make of *Caelica* a more complete record of an individual's experiences than had been any of the cycles' predecessors.

The contrast between the two loves of sonnets 84 and 85 is one of substantiality and insubstantiality. While Cupid's power in sonnet 84 had always been linked to the allure of females, love in the second poem is "Perfections spirit, Goddesse of the minde." Earthly love is, as sonnet 84 had emphasized, mutable, but heavenly love is

> Constant, because it sees no cause to varie,
> A Quintessence of Passions overthrowne,
> Rais'd above all that change of objects carry,
> A Nature by no other nature knowne;
>   For Glorie's of eternitie a frame,
>   That by all bodies else obscures her name.

Immutable and radiant, divine love surrounds man's flickering existence; it is "the first and last in us that is alive." In the tormented syntax of the last two lines, one learns that as soon as the glory of love passes from the eternal to the temporal it is

marred and obscured. Only as man renounces the temporal and
strives toward the eternal will he be able to participate in this
supernature of the spirit. The dualism presented by this poem is,
of course, the same dualism present in the plays and the treatises,
although only in *Of Religion* does Greville go as far as he does
here in choosing definitively between them. The choice is, as
Thom Gunn has said, not solely a matter of rejection, for in the
acceptance of divine love there is a sense of fulfillment, a unifying
of self with a harmonious eternity.[5]

Sonnet 85 would seem to indicate that this choice can be made
with relative calm and equanimity. Greville may very well have
wanted his subsequent religious lyrics to share this serene tone,
but this was not to be possible. His was far too anxious and
gloomy a temperament to retain this calmness for long, and, indeed, as soon as sonnet 86 he is *in extremis.* While sonnet 85 had
been almost devoid of imagery, sonnet 86 is full of images of tur-
bulent agitation. Greville returns to the vast universal setting that
had distinguished some of his best poems in the first part of the
cycle.

> The Earth with thunder torne, with fire blasted,
> With waters drowned, with windie palsey shaken
> Cannot for this with heaven be distasted,
> Since thunder, raine and winds from earth are taken:
> Man torne with Love, with inward furies blasted,
> Drown'd with despaire, with fleshly lustings shaken,
> Cannot for this with heaven be distasted,
> Love, furie, lustings out of man are taken.
> Then Man, endure thy selfe, those clouds will vanish;
> Life is a Top which whipping Sorrow driveth;
> Wisdome must beare what our flesh cannot banish,
> The humble leade, the stubborne bootlesse striveth:
>   Or Man, forsake thy selfe, to heaven turne thee,
>   Her flames enlighten Nature, never burne thee.

The poem is in many respects a logical, if not tonal, continuation
of sonnet 85. In that poem the soul was called upon to move forward from the body to the heavens, and in this one the necessity
for, as well as the perils of, that journey are made clear. The
violence in the universe of a world torn by nature is made
analogous to the less visible but just as deadly harm done to the
little world of man by his own propensities for earthly love, fury,

and lust. Man's tendency is to blame heaven for his misery, but, as Waswo has pointed out, Greville gives man no more justification for doing so here than he did in sonnet 16 where, it will be recalled, a similar situation existed.[6] The analogy with a chaotic earth demands that the causes of violence be looked for in the interior of macrocosm and microcosm alike, with heaven sharing no responsibility in the matter.

Two responses to this human dilemma are presented in the sestet. The first is that of stoic endurance, an alternative that there is no reason to doubt Greville had often found attractive. He had, in fact, counseled his reader in the *Letter to an Honourable Lady* in very much these terms. But there is another alternative available now, and its succinct formulation in the structurally emphatic position of the couplet makes it quite clearly the preferred remedy. From the fire of earthly passion the reader is encouraged to move to the cleansing and illuminating flame of divine love. The need for heavenly grace is obvious in the poem, and the freedom with which it will be given if only man will "turn" himself to receive it lends to the conclusion of the sonnet an affirmation that would have been difficult to anticipate in the octave.

Such moments of spiritual optimism are present in this series of poems, although the prevalent mood is considerably darker. In sonnet 87 he stays with the morbid and the mordant in a representation of and commentary on the death scene of a sinner:

> When as Mans life, the light of humane lust,
> In socket of his earthly lanthorne burnes,
> That all this glory unto ashes must,
> And generation to corruption turnes;
>> Then fond desires that onely feare their end,
>> Doe vainely wish for life, but to amend.

The continuation of the flame image from the final line of sonnet 86 is appropriate, for the illumination from the guttering candle of the dying man's life is the symbolic opposite of the eternal heavenly flame. The essence of the poem is ironic criticism, criticism in the couplet of the first stanza of the universal wish at the moment of death to have done things differently in life and criticism in the couplet of the second and final stanza of the fearfully curious men who want to know the details of how a fellow sinner "left his breath." The time for avoiding such distresses is, of course, the repentant life that precedes death, but the poem implicitly acknowledges man's disinclination to amend his life while time remains. Only when it is too late, and then with the wrong motives, does he attempt to avoid the awful horror of the cessation of existence.

Sonnet 88 further delineates the proper attitudes for repentance, this time specifying intellectual lapses in need of correction. Man's error, it would seem, is one of an excess of mental curiosity, and he needs to be instructed as to the proper limits of his intelligence:

> Man, dreame no more of curious mysteries,
> As what was here before the world was made,
> The first Mans life, the state of Paradise,
> Where heaven is, or hells eternall shade,
>   For Gods works are like him, all infinite;
>   And curious search, but craftie sinnes delight.

The point is identical to Raphael's admonition to Adam in *Paradise Lost* to "be lowly wise" and, indeed, to the less lyrical formulation that Greville himself makes in *Humane Learning*. Speculation about the unknowable will require an expenditure of time and energy that could better be invested in one's personal salvation. This position should not be taken as willful obscurantism; rather, it is a very precise spelling out of what are to Greville crucial priorities.

After enumerating various Old Testament calamities, some of them, like the Flood, global in scope and all of them affecting large numbers of people, he subordinates them as being "nothing" when compared to "the mans renewed birth" to be brought about by repentance: "First, let the Law plough up thy wicked heart, / That Christ may come, and all these types depart." Following the customary Renaissance interpretation of the Old Testament by which many events become precursive analogues or "types" of later events in Christian history, Greville daringly suggests that all of the scriptural happenings that he has named occurred as prototypes of the revolution that takes place in the individual soul at the moment of spiritual conversion. The "Law" that will work to destroy personal wickedness has been explained by Peterson as a tenet of Calvinist doctrine that had become a part of Anglican orthodoxy by the time Greville wrote the poem. Law, in this sense, reminds man that he deserves nothing better than death as a consequence of his sins while withholding from him the actual fact of death. When man's reflections have rendered him properly sorrowful he will also come to understand that his hating his sins is the first step in the acceptance of Christ's infinite mercy.[7] Thus the Old Testament types become "nothing" in another sense too, for they, in their mere destructiveness, are highly inadequate models of the positive regeneration that can follow destruction in the Christian's soul.

The third stanza concludes the poem on a quieter, more intimate note:

> When thou hast swept the house that all is cleare,
> When thou the dust hast shaken from thy feete,
> When Gods All-might doth in thy flesh appeare,
> Then Seas with streames above thy skye doe meet;
>   For Goodnesse onely doth God comprehend,
>   Knowes what was first, and what shall be the end.

In its images of humble domesticity, this stanza approaches the mood of some of Herbert's finest lyrics. It returns the poem to the theme introduced in the opening lines, reminding the reader that to know God, to know the All-Knowing, is the highest possible knowledge. Waswo points to the grammatical ambiguity of "onely" by which Greville "indicates both the error of Man's prideful attempts to understand the eternal (only God knows first and last) as well as the moral direction such attempts must properly take (God comprehends only goodness)."[8] To suggest this latter idea is, of course, to suggest a greater capacity for goodness in man than is usually the case with Greville, but for the truly regenerate souls all is possible, if not on earth then certainly in heaven.

The next poem continues the emphasis of stanza two in sonnet 88 on the Law as the effecting agent of repentance. This poem takes up two possible responses to the Law, shows both to be fallacious, and concludes with a demonstration of the absolute subjugation that the Law requires. The first response was that of the early heretical sect of Manicheans who held that God was insubstantial and that therefore Christ's life on earth was merely

imaginary. The contrasting response is the modern one that
Greville describes in the next stanza, a response for which modern
Christians congratulate themselves but which Greville ironically
suggests may be just as inaccurate as that of the Manicheans:

> We seeme more inwardly to know the Sonne,
> And see our owne salvation in his blood:
> When this is said, we thinke the worke is done,
> And with the Father hold our portion good:
> As if true life within these words were laid,
> For him that in life, never words obey'd.

If the Manicheans put too little faith in substance, the modern
"believer" puts too much faith in words, in the supposed capacity
of words to make rational sense of the miracle of the atonement.
Greville's dissatisfaction with the comfort of this kind of religion
becomes evident in the final stanza:

> If this be safe, it is a pleasant way,
> The Crosse of Christ is very easily borne:
> But six dayes labour makes the sabboth day,
> The flesh is dead before grace can be borne.
> The heart must first beare witnesse with the
> booke,
> The earth must burne, ere we for Christ can looke.

The Law that in the previous poem is depicted as an active force
in human affairs is here once again the origin of unrelenting
demands. The recurrent flame image is now the fire of the apo-
calypse that will precede the second coming of Christ. This will
be one obvious manifestation of the Law, but, prior to that, the
Law must also work its way in the smaller domain of the individual heart. More than mere verbal understanding is at issue
here; there must be a total crushing of the spirit of sin before the
concomitant acceptance of God's grace can begin. Faith must be
uncomfortably visceral as well as coolly cerebral.

It would be wrong to dwell too long on the threatening aspects
of some of these poems. True, the ominous warnings of perdition's suffering are present, but Greville's emphasis is usually on
this life rather than on what lies beyond death. We need not doubt
that he wanted to believe in the orthodox version of futurity, but
often such a futurity seems for him to be incomprehensible to the

mortal mind, even to the vision of the poet. The consequence of this is that his attention falls on the moment of conversion in man's present life, and God's power is more threatening for the spiritual anguish that the unregenerate will undergo while he is still alive than after he is dead. His dilemma in these final poems is that he never seems completely convinced that his repentance has been sufficient for God's demands. The divine grace to which he alludes frequently enough can never quite illuminate his dark night of the soul. His typical attitude is one of praying, hoping, and waiting nervously.

Greville's inability or disinclination in this section of *Caelica* to escape completely from his position in mortality may provide the explanation for the existence of the poems with a social or political orientation. The facts of his biography show clearly that he remained an active courtier to the very end, and this interest in how man lives in the world remains present even within a series of meditative poems. One such poem, sonnet 91, was examined at the beginning of this chapter. It is in many respects typical of the content and tone of sonnets 90 through 97 where the moral concerns of the self are dealt with in the context of their universal applicability to the situations of other men. Sonnet 94 is another such example, treating, as it does, the theme of man's greed to add one pleasant experience to another, to "multiply desire" like a dishonest bankteller or like a young girl who gathers more flowers than she possibly can need with the consequence that the first-picked blooms on the bottom of her basket wither and are crushed by the weight of those picked later. The lesson to be learned here is that self-indulgence in pleasures can lead only to a counterproductive sense of frustration as the pleasure-seeker discovers that satiety deprives him both of present happiness and the memories of past joys. The remedy for the situation is twofold, one part supplied by man and the other by God. Man can fix his sights, if he wants to, solely on "good desires," those that presumably are least worldly, while God will insure that man will not have his own way completely in any case: "For lest Man should thinke flesh a seat of blisse, / God workes that his joy mixt with sorrow is." Although this conclusion comes as an interesting and effective surprise in the poem, the idea that it sets forth can hardly stun anyone who has read any of Greville's other mature work. Rarely, we suppose, did he ever imagine "flesh" to be a "seat of blisse."

The possibility of human happiness is held out once again in one half of the duality examined in sonnet 95. The poem offers an analysis of the apparently contradictory passions of malice and love. Greville points out their dissimilarity but also suggests an essential identity of effect for the holders of the emotions:

> Both raging most, when they be most withstood:
>   Though enemies, yet doe in this agree,
>   That both still breake the hearts where in they be.

A stanza is given over to the evils of malice and another to the raptures of love, but Greville encounters structural difficulties when he attempts to summarize and once again join together the two halves of his theme. After brief statements in which he aligns malice with the devil's party and love with that of the angels, he closes with a sudden expansion of his subject to the world of politics: "Tyrants through feare and malice feed on blood, / Good Kings secure at home, seeke all mens good." It would be difficult enough to carry the reader through from a general discussion of how the qualities affect all men to the very particular application of the attitudes to kings, but Greville makes even more problems for himself by failing to apply the qualities in a particularly understandable way. Apparently the good kings exemplify love, but the comparison to the malice of tyrants ignores the subtle similarities of the passions that have been brought out elsewhere in the poem.

Sonnet 96 is crucial in several respects to the development of this section of the sonnet cycle. The longest poem in the section, it also shows a heavier use of poetic imagery than do most of the others. In part this increased richness of diction can be attributed to Greville's examination in the poem of the seductiveness of nature and of the excited responses of man to the bounties that Nature apparently offers him. These appeals of the world are precisely the dangers that Greville has been presenting in the immediately preceding poems, and these are the appeals that will have to be decisively rejected before the greater glories of supernature can become apparent to man.

The poem traces the path through life taken by the repentant man, beginning with his initial sensual delight in pleasure:

> In those yeeres, when our Sense, Desire and Wit,
>   Combine, that Reason shall not rule the heart;

> Pleasure is chosen as a Goddesse fit,
> The wealth of Nature freely to impart.

Greville's usual pronoun usage in these poems is a generalized third-person "he" or "they" to suit his sweeping statements about the nature of "man." It is therefore significant that he chooses to open this poem with the more intimate first-person plural "our," although the significance of that change cannot fully be appreciated until we reach the full intimacy of the "I" in sonnets 98 and 99. What "we" have chosen in this description is a pleasure that at first seems delightful but which the rest of the stanza denigrates as being merely an "Idoll" whose beauty is greater from "further off" than it is upon closer inspection: "Lost onely, or made lesse by perfect knowing." Waswo has pointed to the Platonic implications of the statement, for, like Plato, Greville consistently finds the world and its adornments to be perverted and false as the shadows on the walls of Plato's cave.[9] Pleasure has no real wealth to impart because nature is bankrupt of substance and value.

The next two stanzas describe some of the more immediate consequences of man's indulgence in pleasure, that "faire Usurper" who "runnes a Rebels way." Man thinks that his enjoyment is complete, but this is self-delusion since his urges and his gratifications are always transitory. Man is compared to an ignorant satyr who tries to kiss the fire because of its "faire appearing light" only to be burned by a force that he cannot understand behind the appearance. The eventual outcome of a life of attempts at pleasure is a confusion similar to the satyr's. Man knows that something has gone wrong, but he is uncertain as to what it is:

> So his affections carries on, and casts
> In declination to the errour still;
>   As by the truth he gets no other light,
>   But to see Vice, a restlesse infinite.

In the final three stanzas of the poem, Greville traces the path of regeneration for such men. As the restlessness with the world continues, it leads eventually to a profound spiritual depression in which the individual has "exiled, waved, or disgraced" all of the "hypocrisies of fraile humanity." But it is a necessary depression, for it is the precondition of spiritual revival: "Whence from the

depth of fatall desolation, / Springs up the height of his
Regeneration."

The argument of the lyric is a condensed form of the theology
that is worked out at greater length in the treatises, especially *Of
Religion*. Man's spring from the nadir of desolation to the height
of regenerate bliss is a transition from the world to God. The
pagan Platonic philosophy that causes Greville to reject the shams
of the world is useful but also limited. It can make man acutely
aware of his condition, but awareness is of little comfort. Comfort must come from the grace of a Christian God, with certain
minimal contributions from man to his own cause:

> His sixe dayes labour past, and that cleere staire,
> Figure of Sabboths rest, rais'd by this fall;
>   For God comes not till man be overthrowne;
>   Peace is the seed of grace, in dead flesh sowne.

Man can mortify his own flesh and be receptive to God's grace,
but Greville's God is, as usual, the God of Calvin and therefore
dispenses rest and reward to men who cannot possibly deserve it
in their roles as mortals. Greville's final stanza emphasizes and
reemphasizes this point as it moves through a series of images that
define the sinfulness and unmeriting qualities of worldly flesh, a
"living-dead thing, till it be new borne." His final definition for it
is gloomy in the extreme: "A boat, to which the world it selfe is
Sea, / Wherein the minde sayles on her fatall way." No earthly
good can come of such a voyage, but then Greville had never until this poem gone farther in rejecting mundane concerns as
creators either of good or of ill.

The poet returns to the themes of sonnets 88 and 89 in sonnet
97, taking up once again what he terms the necessity for the Law
to "plow up" the human heart before the full effect of the gospel
can be felt. But in sonnet 97, by staying with the first-person
plural pronouns introduced in the previous poem and by multi-
plying their use, he gives an added urgency to the notion that "the
flesh is dead before grace can be borne" (sonnet 89). This twenty-
two-line poem begins as a prayer to "eternall Truth, almighty, infinite," although by the poem's midpoint that particular putative
auditor drops out and the meditation on man's unwillingness to
respond completely to the divine imperatives for repentance is
directed to the sinner rather than to God. "One thought to God

wee give, the rest to sinne / Quickely unbent is all desire of good"
encapsulates the spirit of the concluding lines of the poem, as
Greville becomes steadily more acerbic on his topic. There is present in the lyric an obsessive sense of guilt for spiritual, if not actual, participation in the crucifixion of Christ:

> Wee pray to Christ, yet helpe to shed his blood . . .
> We with the Jewes even Christ still crucifie,
> As not yet come to our impiety.

This guilt should, and in Greville's case obviously does, inhibit
any sense of calm that the "believer" might possess as a result of
having fulfilled the outward and verbal forms of religion. Such a
calm is a false calm, and it must be banished as relentlessly as
overt sin is banished.

The poem affords a good example of Greville's poetic style and
manner in the mature lyrics. It is a style toward which he had
been moving throughout the love poems in *Caelica* from the time
when he had decided that the Petrarchism that had been so effectively used and modulated by Sidney was simply uncongenial and
inappropriate to his pen. These early attempts at smooth lyricism
and consciously "poetic" imagery had been replaced, as has been
shown, by a sparer, more conversational style that better fits the
disillusionment with love that came into the cycle poem by poem.
In the famous passage from the *Life of Sidney*, he had made an
accurate distinction between his poems and those of his friend:
"For my own part, I found my creeping Genius more fixed upon
the Images of Life, than the Images of Wit. . . ."[10] The distinction is a general one, applied to all aspects of their poetry, but it
shows especially accurate insight on the issue of differences in
style. The "images of life" of which Greville wrote came increasingly to him to require expression in a style that was more and
more devoid of traditional adornment. His statements in *Of
Humane Learning* justifying his praxis, arguing for a severity and
spareness in poetic diction, do not, perhaps, seem as striking to a
modern reader as they would have to Greville's contemporaries
whose tastes had been molded by Petrarch, Seneca, and the other
ornate stylists. When he began devoting his poetic energies to
religious themes (themes that, by the way, had rarely been dealt
with directly by earlier Renaissance lyricists), he seems to have
felt even more strongly the necessity for stripping poetry down to

its verbal essentials. The impulse is in large part governed by the theology of Greville's radical protestantism with its emphasis on unadorned expressiveness in all communication. This plainness has commonly been observed to be a point of distinction between styles of preaching, but what Kenneth Murdock says of pulpit style in this summary is strikingly applicable to the attitude that lies behind Greville's verse:

> The Puritan's earthy phrases and images, his restriction of his material to that supplied by the Bible or the everyday life of his audience, his seriousness of purpose, and his willingness to admit only those rhetorical devices and "similitudes" which served to drive home or to make more intelligible what he saw as the truth, were all directly related to his view of God and of man. The realism and concreteness of his work, the firmness of its structure, and its dignity of tone, all reflect the profound conviction from which it came.[11]

One consequence of such an attitude is, of course, the negation of the value of all literature and the stifling of all creative impulses. It cannot be doubted that just this point of view was held by most of Greville's Calvinist contemporaries, and that there is something essentially self-contradictory about the concept of "Puritan poetry." Prior to Milton (who is hardly a typical Puritan in any case), the quantity of Puritan imaginative literature is small indeed.

Theology alone does not, however, provide the full explanation for the existence of Greville's style, or, to put the matter somewhat differently, there are other implications to the style than the purely theological. What came to be called the "plain style" probably would have developed at the opening of the seventeenth century without any religious impetus. Wesley Trimpi has described the progress of Ben Jonson toward this style for goals that were principally aesthetic in nature.[12] A reaction against the ornateness (or what was perceived as ornateness) in the style of poets such as Sidney and Spenser, the plain style was thought of as the fittest mode for the expression of the truth, be it religious or secular. Yvor Winters, the first and in some ways the most important modern apologist for the plain style, has described its qualities in the hands of its best practitioners, in whose number he counts Greville:

Only a master of style can deal in a plain manner with obvious matter: we are concerned with the kind of poetry which is perhaps the hardest to

compose and the last to be recognized, a poetry not striking nor original as
to subject, but merely true and universal, that is, in a sense, commonplace; not striking nor original in rhetorical procedure, but economical
and efficient; a poetry which permits itself originality, that is, the breath
of life, only in the most restrained subtleties of diction and of cadence, but
which by virtue of those subtleties inspires its universals with their full
value as experience.[13]

In a poem such as sonnet 97, Greville gives the reader just the
combination of which Winters speaks: universal ideas set forth in
restrained diction. There is an aphoristic quality to lines such as
"One thought to God wee give, the rest to sinne, / Quickely unbent is all desire of good." In his word choice Greville gravitates,
as usual, toward abstraction with a sudden enlivening provided
by a verb such as "unbent" which can give form to abstractions.
The poem's rhythm is stately but with subtle variations. There is
metric agitation in the first line of the couplet ("We with the
Jewes even Christ still crucifie, / As not yet come to our impiety")
with its extra syllable, and five strong accents before the iambic
smoothness of the last line. The change in rhythm supports the
sense of the couplet with its anguish of the realization of the
speaker's share in the crucifixion, an anguish which in turn gives
way to the quiet acceptance of his remaining ignorant of the full
extent of his sin.

The appearance of the "I" at long last in the religious poems
would give sonnet 98 special distinction in any case. But it is
made even more noteworthy by its presentation of the poet at the
rock-bottom of his spiritual state. He is here only a step from complete despair:

> Wrapt up, O Lord, in mans degeneration;
> The glories of thy truth, thy joyes eternall,
> Reflect upon my soul darke desolation,
> And ugly prospects o're the sprites infernall.
>   Lord, I have sinn'd, and mine iniquity,
>   Deserves this hell; yet Lord deliver me.
>
> Thy power and mercy never comprehended,
> Rest lively imag'd in my Conscience wounded:
> Mercy to grace, and power to feare extended,
> Both infinite, and I in both confounded;
>   Lord, I have sinn'd, and mine iniquity,
>   Deserves this hell, yet Lord deliver me.

If from this depth of sinne, this hellish grave,
And fatall absence from my Saviours glory,
I could implore his mercy, who can save,
And for my sinnes, not paines of sinne, be sorry:
    Lord, from this horror of iniquity,
    And hellish grave, thou wouldst deliver me.

The knowledge of his own sin that he has gained steadily in the meditations of the previous poems has here left him virtually paralyzed in a state of hyper-awareness. It is cool comfort to him to know that his sins are not unique ("mans degeneration"), for he nevertheless suffers from a sense of spiritual isolation ("darke desolation") from all other creatures, mortal or divine. His dilemma, as Peterson has observed, is the dilemma of Luther and Calvin—how a God who should extend only rigorous justice to him can also be a God of mercy.[14] He acknowledges that he has never understood this paradox, and, in some ways, it seems that he never will. He is at this point close to what Waswo has called "the uniquely Christian despair that results from a profound conviction of guilt" and to which Spenser's Redcrosse Knight succumbs in book 1 of *The Faerie Queene* when he has to be saved from suicide.[15] Such guilt is a necessary part of repentance, but the sinner must somehow move past it to an acceptance of God's mercy.

The possibility of making sense of the relationship between justice and mercy is presented in a highly qualified way in the "If . . ." clause of the third stanza. The grammatical resolution of that clause in the poem's final line gives an assurance of salvation on two conditions: the penitent's capacity to overcome what is presumably an excess of human pride in order to ask for mercy and his decision to hate his sins and their causes rather than the torments that he suffers in life that are their consequences. Only by taking these steps will he be able to render himself a fit recipient of God's mercy. This participation in the process of redemption from sin is reminiscent of the elaboration of that process in *A Treatise of Religion* and is, as was noted in the discussion of that treatise, divergent from the unilateral deliverance of grace in thoroughgoing Calvinism. One unstated result of sorrow for the causes of sin is the amending of one's life to remove these causes. Greville in no way stresses this point, but it may reasonably be assumed that when he wrote this poem he had not

yet reached the utter pessimism on the efficacy of human resolution and action that marked his final years and that he still was
desirous of making himself into a fitter image of his creator.

The anguish that Greville puts himself through in these meditations is manifested again in sonnet 99, a poem which shows some
spiritual advancement over its predecessor:

> Downe in the depth of mine iniquity,
> That ugly center of infernall spirits;
> Where each sinne feeles her owne deformity,
> In these peculiar torments she inherits,
>> Depriv'd of humane graces, and divine,
>> Even there appeares this saving God of mine.
>
> And in this fatall mirrour of transgression,
> Shewes man as fruit of his degeneration,
> The errours ugly infinite impression,
> Which beares the faithlesse downe to desperation;
>> Depriv'd of humane graces and divine,
>> Even there appeares this saving God of mine.
>
> In power and truth, Almighty and eternall,
> Which on the sinne reflects strange desolation,
> With glory scourging all the Sprites infernall,
> And uncreated hell with unprivation;
>> Depriv'd of humane graces, not divine,
>> Even there appeares this saving God of mine.
>
> For on this sp'rituall Crosse condemned lying,
> To paines infernall by eternall doome,
> I see my Saviour for the same sinnes dying,
> And from that hell I fear'd, to free me, come;
>> Depriv'd of humane graces, not divine,
>> Thus hath his death rais'd up this soule of mine.

Waswo has made an interesting comparison of this poem and
Herbert's "Love (III)." Both lyrics treat the same theme: a Christian penitent feels undeserving of redemption until he comes to
understand the significance of Christ's sacrifice for his sins. But it
is hard to imagine two more different poems tonally on this subject. Herbert's poem is set in the form of a homely dialogue between the sinner and God. Even though the sinner seems fully

convinced of his unworthiness, his sense of guilt finds gentle
expression as he calls himself not "worthy," "unkinde," and "un-
grateful"—nothing stronger. It is always apparent in this lyric
that he will be saved, a knowledge that finds fruition in the closing lines when the speaker, cast as a weary traveler, accepts the
atonement of Christ:

> And Know you not, sayes Love, who bore the blame?
> My deare, then I will serve.
> You must sit down, sayes Love, and taste my meat:
> So I did sit and eat.

Waswo contrasts the differences in levels of anxiety between the
two poems in terms of the differences in religious climate between
Herbert's assured Anglicanism and Greville's far sterner Calvinism.[16] For Greville, thinking of God as the host of a rural inn is
a complete impossibility, and if grace can eventually be accepted,
it cannot be done with the same easy, witty cleverness that
Herbert displays. Greville's dark night of the soul must be lifted
with the same forcefulness that distinguished its descent, and
God's wrath cannot be mitigated by poetic symbol.

As was the case in sonnet 98, Greville's self has become its own
private hell in this poem. The spatial energy of the poem's opening is all centripetal as the reader is pulled downward into the
poet's "ugly center of infernall spirits" to share his perspective on
sin as it transforms itself into its own punishment. One of the
principal achievements of the poem is the way in which it exercises and maintains this spatial control over the reader, generally
holding him in this center but in each stanza's refrain opening up
a vision of a God who is outside of the self and in the final refrain
moving the soul of poet and audience upward and outward from
the self to the domain of the deity.

The sense of captivity in the poem is reinforced by Greville's
manipulation of rhyme and meter. He frequently is given to using
a double rhyme of two syllables at the ends of his lines, but no
poem makes as striking use of the technique as does this one.
Thom Gunn has plausibly suggested that the calculated effect of
the double rhymes is to convey a sense of self-imposed difficulty,
of the strain that is inevitable when someone meditates on the sinfulness of his own nature.[17] This sense is certainly here, created
not only by the rhymes but also by a distillation of all the other

techniques that distinguish Greville's religious verse—powerful, tearing alliteration, assonance that adds significant quantitative length to many of the syllables, and a careful modulation of meaning in the pattern established by the refrain.

The refrain is, in fact, the element of the poem that most directly controls the progress of its theme. The change of "and" to "not" in stanza three, a change that is further reinforced in stanza four, serves to divide the poem into halves with the second half taking on increasing affirmation as it moves from third to fourth stanzas. The refrain does tend to move at a somewhat faster rate than the rest of the poem in this regard, since it is not until the third and fourth lines of the final stanza that the discursive statement that the poem makes gives any indication of a reconciliation with God. In the third stanza the poet has witnessed Christ's scourging of Hell after the crucifixion and the consequent transformation of negative into positive ("uncreated hell with unprivation"), although he as yet has not perceived the applicability of this power and this act to his own situation. But in the third line of the fourth stanza the first use in the poem of the nominative case "I" signals the sudden, but hard-won, comprehension of the selfless generosity of Christ. The poet is still a wretch, still "depriv'd of human graces," but divine grace has at last released him from his psychological self-imprisonment.

After sonnet 99 the ten poems that remain in the cycle are considerably more miscellaneous in nature than are those that have directly preceded them. Some turn the reader's attention outward toward society and whatever slight hopes remain for improving its ills, while others remain focused on Greville's vision of the condition of his soul. Sonnet 100 is an acute rendering of the psychological state of fear, be it fear of unseen dangers in the night or fear of one's unseen, confused inner self:

> In Night when colours all to blacke are cast,
> Distinction lost, or gone downe with the light;
> The eye a watch to inward senses plac'd,
> Not seeing, yet still having power of sight,
>
> Gives vaine Alarums to the inward sense,
> Where feare stirr'd up with witty tyranny,
> Confounds all powers, and thorough selfe-offence,
> Doth forge and raise impossibility:

Such as in thicke depriving darkenesses,
Proper reflections of the errour be,
And images of selfe-confusednesses,
Which hurt imaginations onely see;
    And from this nothing seene, tels newes of devils,
    Which but expressions be of inward evils.

The equation that the poem makes between night fears and moral fears is probably somewhat more than metaphoric in terms of Renaissance psychology which would have made a fairly direct connection between scares in the dark and a sense of spiritual damnation. Whatever one's belief on this point might be, there is an undeniable accuracy to the description in the first eight lines of the jumpy confusion that accompanies utter darkness. This state, as Gunn has said, is that of the mind operating on its own, without outside assistance, subjected only to its own "witty tyranny."[18] There is no assistance from the sense perceptions facilitated by daylight and no help from the inner light provided by God.

The sestet of the sonnet suggests, in syntax that is contorted but generally intelligible, that there is a parallel between night fears and the terrors of hell, that one anticipates the other, or in an even more interesting sense, that the devils of hell *are* the "inward evils" that prompt all types of personal anguish. This notion of one's being one's own hell was, of course, present in the previous poem, but here it is presented even more directly. The implication is that often, especially during daylight, man is able to repress the reality of his sin and the consequent anguish that emerges to confront him at night.

Sonnet 102 with its thirteen six-line stanzas is discursive rather than lyrical and is in many respects reminiscent of the verse treatises. Greville allows himself more space in this poem than in the other religious poems in *Caelica* in an effort to make rational sense of the existence and the effects of sin—sin in himself, to be sure, but now also in mankind in general. Although the poem's opening makes the obligatory connection between Adam's original fall and an external serpent, Greville's initial opinion seems to be that sin was largely generated by man himself in his foolish desire to "exceed his God" and to "know more than hee was created to." This, of course, is one of the themes of *Humane Knowledge*, and here Greville takes it up again, dwelling especially on the prototypical instance as a means of explaining how "immortall life, made for mans good, / Is since become the hell of flesh and blood."

But to describe *what* has happened does not adequately respond to the question of *why* matters came to this turn, and it is on the issue of man's motive that Greville reaches a philosophical impasse. Why, if God is perfect, should any aspect of creation have within it the seeds and, later, the fruit of imperfection? The answer comes with the recollection of that antecedent revolt of some of the angels:

> Where did our being then seeke out privation?
> Above, within, without us all was pure,
> Onely the Angels from their discreation,
> By smart declar'd no being was secure,
>   But that transcendent Goodnesse which subsists,
>   By forming and reforming what it lists.

These malign spirits, "refined by their high places in creation," have clear advantages over man in their capacity for "craft and malice." Man, believing naively that all is permitted, that in a state where all is perfect and without sin there similarly "no law could be," is easy prey for the angry fallen spirits. Until this last point, the poem could well have served Milton as an outline to the composition of *Paradise Lost* fifty years later. But Milton, with his emphasis on man's free will and man's clear understanding of God's commands, could hardly have accepted this notion of man's igorance of the concept of law with which the poem concludes:

> And as all finite things seeke infinite,
> From thence deriving what beyond them is;
> So man was led by charmes of this darke sp'rit,
> Which hee could not know till hee did amisse;
>   To trust those Serpents, who learn'd since they fell,
>   Knew more than we did; even their own made hell.
>
> Which crafty oddes made us those clouds imbrace,
> Where sinne in ambush lay to overthrow
> Nature; (that would presume to fadome Grace)
> Or could beleeve what God said was not so:

> Sin, then we knew thee not, and could not hate,
> And now we know thee, now it is too late.

Man is ignorant before the fall and, paradoxically, is still ignorant after his original sin, with one set of limits on his knowledge leading directly to the other. A more bitter temperament than Greville's might at this point have proceeded to an indictment of God for allowing blind, frail mankind to corrupt itself in this way, but Greville carefully stops short of this extreme. The poem expresses sorrow, perhaps even dissatisfaction, over what has happened in human affairs, but any anger is directed at sin rather than at the deity who has allowed man to sin. The line that Greville must walk here and in some of the other final poems is a narrow one, but, as Waswo has argued, Greville's Christian faith, while sometimes anguished, is so scrupulous that there is not even an implicit grudging against God's divine wisdom.[19] There is no point, Greville suggests in this poem and elsewhere, in complaining about a sinful world that cannot be restored to its primal purity. One must instead do what he can with what limited faith, intellect, and energy that he possesses.

That Greville slowly came to relinquish this interest in such worldly activity has been a recurrent theme of this book. The difficulty of dating his works precisely makes it nearly impossible to say at exactly what moment he gave up hope for the world. It seems probable that sonnet 109, the final poem in *Caelica*, was his last piece of imaginative literature and that he wrote it in the final years of his life. But even if it could somehow be established that it had been written somewhat earlier than that, no one could question Greville's wisdom in setting it at the end of the cycle. In its apocalyptic vision of the earth destroyed, it both epitomizes the most effective imagery of the cycle as well as brings to a conclusion Greville's series-long struggle between the claims of God and the claims of the world:

> Syon lyes waste, and thy Jerusalem,
> O Lord, is falne to utter desolation,
> Against thy Prophets, and thy holy men,
> The sinne hath wrought a fatall combination,
>   Prophan'd thy name, thy worship overthrowne,
>   And made thee living Lord, a God unknowne.

Thy powerfull lawes, thy wonders of creation,
Thy Word incarnate, glorious heaven, darke hell,
Lye shadowed under Mans degeneration,
Thy Christ still crucifi'd for doing well,
  Impiety, O Lord, sits on thy throne,
  Which makes thee living Light, A God unknown.

Mans superstition hath thy truths entomb'd,
His Atheisme againe her pomps defaceth,
That sensuall unsatiable vaste wombe
Of thy seene Church, thy unseene Church disgraceth;
  There lives no truth with them that seem thine own,
  Which makes thee living Lord, a God unknowne.

Yet unto thee Lord (mirrour of transgression)
Wee, who for earthly Idols, have forsaken
Thy heavenly Image (sinlesse pure impression)
And so in nets of vanity lye taken,
  All desolate implore that to thine owne,
  Lord, thou no longer live a God unknowne.

Yet Lord let Israels plagues not be eternall,
Nor sinne for ever cloud thy sacred Mountaines,
Nor with false flames spirituall but infernall,
Dry up thy mercies ever springing fountaines,
  Rather, sweet Jesus, fill up time and come,
  To yeeld the sinne her everlasting doome.

The magnificence of the poem has been praised by every critic who has written on it. The modulation of rhythm, the rigor and solemnity of the double rhymes, the variation of the refrain save for the predictable power of the last phrase, all combine here with a literal statement of the greatest import to fulfill one of the principal functions of poetry: the presentation of ideas in a forceful and memorable way. There is no longer present any reluctance to believe in the totality of sin's control over the world. Greville here recoils in terror as he accepts the dominance of sin and pleads with God to annihilate the continuing corruption of His creation.

Especially singled out here, as in *Of Religion*, is the visible church, the organization that allegedly carries forward God's will. But here, in a line of shocking effect, the "seene Church" is characterized only by its "sensuall unsatiable vaste wombe" that disgraces the "unseene Church" of the elect. Whether or not Greville considered himself to be part of this elect is obscure here, as it is everywhere in his references to it. That he would like to be is evident; indeed, the entire poem is written from the perspective of someone disgraced (perhaps literally) by organized religion. But Greville is presumably also among the "wee" who lie tangled in the "nets of vanity" and who must "implore" God for closer knowledge of Him.

It is this refrain of "a God unknowne" that finally proves to be the most haunting element of the poem. Its absence in the last stanza might be taken as a sign that God is no longer unknown to the speaker, but it can hardly be said to have been replaced by anything more affirmative; there is only the plea for the destructive violence of the second coming of Christ. Rather, the reiteration of the unfathomability of the deity only serves to enforce upon the reader more strongly than ever the anguish that Greville experienced whenever he assayed to understand God's ways. The vision and the serenity that seem to have come to the aging Milton never came to him. Unable to find evidence that God would favor him, unwilling to give himself over to despair because of this, Greville lived and died as few men can—by faith alone.

CHAPTER 7

Greville's Current Reputation

THE "what if's" of literary reputation are tantalizing and unanswerable. In Greville's case the "what if" derives from Yvor Winters' statement in 1939 that Greville was "one of the two great masters of the short poem [the other was Ben Jonson] in the Renaissance."[1] As was sometimes unfortunately the case with Winters' polemical dicta, he did not expand very much on the claim, following it only with a brief eight-page survey of *Caelica*. It is my conviction, however, that if Winters had not called attention to Greville in this article on sixteenth-century poetry and in his classroom, Greville's reputation and Greville studies would be much the poorer today. Such was Winters' influence that a sentence from him on any writer could have profound effects on the course of subsequent criticism.

To be sure, even without Winters, Greville would have been noticed. The fine edition of the poems and plays finished by Bullough in 1938 (although not printed until 1945) would have assured that. Furthermore, Rees, in her 1971 critical biography, said that she did not read Winters until her book was completed.[2] But Peterson in 1967, Gunn in 1968, Rebholz in 1971, and Waswo in 1972 all acknowledged their contact with Winters, in print or in class, as the starting point of their interest in Greville's achievement.[3] Their books, in their various ways, go far beyond a mere fleshing-out of Winters' self-consciously contentious argument, but all align themselves essentially with Winters' admiration for Greville's "subtlety and power," for his "concern for his matter and . . . the corresponding indifference to his own personality that [distinguishes him] equally from Sidney and from Donne."[4]

Winters' interest was principally attracted by Greville's accomplishments in the lyric form, and *Caelica* is still the best-known of his works. However, as this study has attempted to show, there has been an increasing amount of attention paid in the last two decades to Greville's efforts in other genres. In part, this has been ancillary to and explanatory of his work as a lyricist, but it has also been undertaken because his longer works, in poetry and in prose, are interesting in themselves. It was in them that Greville found the space for a more systematic development of the thoughts and emotions that had also generated the lyrics, and, as a consequence, it is their articulation of his world view that continues to make Greville a fascinating subject for all who are interested in Renaissance intellectual history.

Still, Greville's current fame must not be overestimated. However powerful Winters' force in the creation of taste, it is clear from a survey of any annual bibliography of work on Renaissance literature that he was not successful (at least, not yet) in convincing the majority of critics of the superiority of Greville's kind of lyric to that of Sidney and Donne. About the most that has been accomplished thus far in most readers of poetry is an awareness of and respect for the austere, even stark, beauties of Greville's later lyrics. It is for this reason that the attention to the longer works that has come from Rebholz, Rees, Maclean, and Wilkes, among others, has been especially valuable in establishing Greville's importance as a thinker of considerable distinction, one whom no scholar of the period can afford to ignore. Greville's works present a view of man's limited hopes and his infinite possibilities for corruption that serves as a necessary corrective to any popular and established impression of a uniformly optimistic Renaissance intellectual climate. It would be surprising if Winters's assertion of Greville's primacy as a poet ever came to be generally accepted. But it is surely true that our own increasingly gloomy age already has found in Greville's thought the harmony of a temperamentally kindred spirit.

Notes and References

Chapter One

1. Sidney, *Defence of Poesie*, in *Miscellaneous Prose*, ed. Katherine Duncan-Jones and Jan van Dorsten (Oxford: Clarendon Press, 1973), p. 110.
2. Richard C. McCoy, *Sir Philip Sidney: Rebellion in Arcadia* (New Brunswick, N.J.: Rutgers University Press, 1979), pp. 23–27. See also F. J. Levy, "Philip Sidney Reconsidered," *English Literary Renaissance*, 2 (1972), 11–15.
3. *The Life of Fulke Greville, First Lord Brooke* (Oxford: Clarendon Press, 1971), p. 9.
4. Ibid., p. 11.
5. Ibid., p. 237.
6. "Fulke Greville: The Courtier as Philosophic Poet," *Modern Language Quarterly*, 33 (1972), 447.
7. Rebholz, pp. 242–43.
8. Quoted in ibid., p. 316.
9. *Poems and Dramas of Fulke Greville, First Lord Brooke*, 2 vols. (New York: Oxford University Press, 1945), I, 34.
10. Waswo, *The Fatal Mirror: Themes and Techniques in the Poetry of Fulke Greville* (Charlottesville: University Press of Virginia, 1972); Farmer, "Holograph Revisions in Two Poems by Fulke Greville," *English Literary Renaissance*, 4 (1974), 98–110.
11. Farmer, p. 108.
12. Rebholz, pp. 341–43.
13. Farmer, p. 108.
14. Cowley's comment is quoted by William Hazlitt, *Complete Works*, ed. P. P. Howe, 21 vols. (London: J. M. Dent, 1931–1934), XVII: 130.
15. *English Literature in the Sixteenth Century* (Oxford: Clarendon Press, 1954), p. 525.
16. "Fulke Greville and the Poetic of the Plain Style," *Texas Studies in Literature and Language*, 11 (1969), 667.

Chapter Two

1. *Sidney's Poetry: Contexts and Interpretations* (1965; reprint ed., New York: W. W. Norton, 1970), pp. 150, 156.
2. *English Literature in the Sixteenth Century*, pp. 327–28.
3. All quotations from *Caelica* will be from Bullough's edition of the poems and dramas. I should note here that in quoting Bullough's text— and, later, in quoting Wilkes' text of some of the treatises, Smith's text of the *Life of Sidney*, and Grosart's text of the *Letter to an Honourable Lady*—I have made certain silent changes: I have modernized the *u/v* and *i/j* printing conventions and I have almost always changed the italic type used to set certain names and phrases to roman.
4. "The Poet as Orator: One Phase of His Judicial Pose" in *The Rhetoric of Renaissance Poetry*, ed. Thomas O. Sloan and Raymond B. Waddington (Berkeley: University of California Press, 1974), p. 20.
5. Waswo, p. 53.
6. "Love's Newfangleness: A Comparison of Greville and Wyatt," *Studies in the Literary Imagination*, 11 (1978), 17.
7. Rebholz, "Love's Newfangleness," p. 21.
8. *Selected Poems of Fulke Greville* (Chicago: University of Chicago Press, 1968), p. 25.
9. Rebholz, *Life*, p. 64.
10. Waswo, pp. 85–86.

Chapter Three

1. Rebholz, p. 329.
2. Rebholz reviews and summarizes the pertinent evidence for the order of the versions on p. 101, n. 42.
3. It should be noted that the 1633 version is the one chosen by Bullough as his copy-text. He includes in an appendix several scenes from the earlier versions that differ substantially from the 1633 text.
4. *Life of Sir Philip Sidney*, ed. Nowell Smith (Oxford: Clarendon Press, 1907), p. 156.
5. For a more detailed study of Seneca's influence here and elsewhere in the sixteenth century, see H. B. Charlton, *The Senecan Tradition in Renaissance Tragedy* (1921; rpt. Folcroft, Pa.: Folcroft Press, 1969).
6. Bullough, ed., *Poems and Dramas*, II, 3.
7. *Life of Sidney*, ed. Smith, pp. 224–25.
8. Bullough, II, 7–25, 40–47.
9. *Fulke Greville, Lord Brooke* (Berkeley: University of California Press, 1971), p. 169.
10. Bullough, II, 58.
11. All citations will be to the text of Bullough's edition.

12. *The Jacobean Drama: An Interpretation*, 4th ed. (London: Methuen, 1958), p. 194.

13. Ure, "Fulke Greville's Dramatic Characters," *Review of English Studies*, 1 (1950), reprinted in Ure, *Elizabethan and Jacobean Drama* (New York: Harper & Row, 1974), p. 112, n.

14. Bullough, II, 45.

15. Bullough, II, 53–58; Rebholz, pp. 101–102, n. 42, 329–331.

16. Rebholz, p. 202.

17. Ibid.

18. Rees, p. 181.

19. See, for example, Ivor Morris, "The Tragic Vision of Fulke Greville," *Shakespeare Survey*, 14 (1961), 66–75, and Jean Jacquot, "Religion et Raison d'Etat dans l'Oeuvre de Fulke Greville," *Etudes Anglaises*, 5 (1952), 211–22.

20. Ure, p. 105.

21. Bullough, II, 34.

22. For the fullest survey of drama written for the social elite, see Alfred Harbage, *Shakespeare and the Rival Traditions* (1952; reprint ed., Bloomington: Indiana University Press, 1970).

23. Bullough, II, 61.

Chapter Four

1. Rebholz, pp. 331–40.

2. Rees, p. 212.

3. Bullough, I, 71–72.

4. The issue of the deletion is discussed by G. A. Wilkes in the introduction to his edition of *The Remains: Being Poems of Monarchy and Religion* (London: Oxford University Press, 1965), pp. 22–23.

5. All citation to *Monarchy* is to Wilkes's edition of *The Remains*.

6. A full discussion of Greville's relationship to contemporary thought on the nature of monarchy is provided by Hugh N. Maclean, "Fulke Greville: Kingship and Sovereignty," *Huntington Library Quarterly*, 16 (1953), 237–71.

7. Maclean, pp. 163–64.

8. Bullough, I, 63.

9. Citation to *Fame and Honor* is to Bullough's edition.

10. Bullough, I, 67.

11. Rebholz, pp. 336–37.

12. Citation to *Wars* is to Bullough's edition.

13. Maclean, "Fulke Greville on War," *Huntington Library Quarterly*, 21 (1958), 105.

14. Ibid., pp. 105–6.

15. Bullough, I, 54.

16. Rebholz, pp. 303, 340.

17. Citation to *Human Learning* is to Bullough's edition.

18. Colie, *Paradoxica Epidemica: The Renaissance Tradition of Paradox* (Princeton: Princeton University Press, 1966), pp. 411–12.

19. Citation to *Religion* is Wilkes's edition in *The Remains*.

20. Waller, "Fulke Greville's Struggle With Calvinism," *Studia Neophilologica*, 44 (1972), 309.

Chapter Five

1. A sizeable number of the letters were printed or paraphrased in the late nineteenth century in the Salisbury volumes of the *Historical Manuscript Commission Reports* devoted to the papers of the Cecil family at Hatfield House.

2. This opinion has been given to me in personal correspondence from Professor Farmer.

3. Rebholz, p. 328; Rees, pp. 175–77.

4. "A Letter to an Honourable Lady" in *The Works . . of Fulke Greville, Lord Brooke*, ed. Alexander B. Grosart (1870; reprint ed., New York: AMS Press, 1966) IV, 282. All future citation to the *Letter* will be to this edition.

5. See Harry Levin, *The Myth of the Golden Age in the Renaissance* (Bloomington: Indiana University Press, 1969).

6. Rebholz, p. 85.

7. "The Argument of Milton's *Comus*," *University of Toronto Quarterly*, 11 (1941), 46–71, and "Nature and Grace in *The Faerie Queene*," *ELH*, 16 (1949), 194–228.

8. Rebholz, p. 76. Rees also reprints the letter, pp. 46–47.

9. Rebholz, pp. 205, 331–36; Rees, p. 57.

10. "Sources and Analogues of the *Life of Sidney*," *Studies in Philology*, 74 (1977), 299.

11. All citation is to Nowell Smith's edition of the *Life*.

12. Caldwell, p. 280.

13. Ibid., p. 288.

14. Ibid., p. 292.

15. Rees, p. 65.

16. Ibid., p. 64.

17. Ibid., p. 51.

Chapter Six

1. Rebholz, pp. 217, 339.

2. Louis L. Martz, *The Poetry of Meditation: A Study in English Religious Literature of the Seventeenth Century*, rev. ed. (New Haven: Yale University Press, 1964).

3. All citation will again be to Bullough's text of *Caelica*.

4. Gary L. Litt, " 'Images of Life': A Study of Narrative and Structure in Fulke Greville's *Caelica*," *Studies in Philology*, 69 (1972), 221.

5. Gunn, pp. 33–35.

6. Waswo, p. 97.

7. Peterson, pp. 272–73.

8. Waswo, p. 114.

9. Ibid., p. 118.

10. *Life of Sidney*, p. 224.

11. *Literature and Theology in Colonial New England* (Cambridge: Harvard University Press, 1949), p. 61; also quoted by Waswo, p. 124.

12. *Ben Jonson's Poems: A Study of the Plain Style* (Stanford: Stanford University Press, 1962).

13. *Forms of Discovery* (Chicago: Alan Swallow, 1967), p. 4.

14. Peterson, p. 282.

15. Waswo, p. 125.

16. Ibid., pp. 139–40.

17. Gunn, p. 37.

18. Ibid., p. 36.

19. Waswo, p. 147.

Chapter Seven

1. The 1939 article was reprinted in *Forms of Discovery*, p. 44.

2. Rees, p. xii.

3. Peterson, p. v; Gunn, pp. 7, 14, n. 1; Rebholz, pp. vii–ix; Waswo, pp. vii, 160–61.

4. Winters, pp. 51–52.

Selected Bibliography

PRIMARY SOURCES

Life of Sir Philip Sidney. Edited by Nowell Smith. Oxford: Clarendon Press, 1907.
Poems and Dramas of Fulke Greville, First Lord Brooke. Edited by Geoffrey Bullough. 2 vols. New York: Oxford University Press, 1945.
The Remains Being Poems of Monarchy and Religion. Edited by G. A. Wilkes. London: Oxford University Press, 1965.
Selected Poems of Fulke Greville. Edited by Thom Gunn. Chicago: University of Chicago Press, 1968.
Selected Writings of Fulke Greville. Edited by Joan Rees. London: Athlone Press, 1973.
The Works in Verse and Prose Complete of the Right Honourable Fulke Greville, Lord Brooke. Edited by Alexander B. Grosart. 4 vols. 1870; reprint ed., New York: AMS Press. 1966.

SECONDARY SOURCES

1. Books:

REBHOLZ, RONALD A. *The Life of Fulke Greville, First Lord Brooke*. Oxford: Clarendon Press, 1971. More social and political than literary, this book, the fullest biography, has occasionally been felt to base its dating of Greville's writings on too-speculative internal evidence.
REES, JOAN. *Fulke Greville, Lord Brooke, 1554–1628*. Berkeley: University of California Press, 1971. Especially good for its tracing of the thematic interrelationships among Greville's works.
WASWO, RICHARD. *The Fatal Mirror: Themes and Techniques in the Poetry of Fulke Greville*. Charlottesville: University Press of Virginia, 1972. A perceptive and detailed reading of the *Caelica* cycle, placing it in its poetic and religious traditions.

2. Articles and Portions of Books:

BENNET, PAULA. "Recent Studies in Greville." *English Literary*

Renaissance, 2 (1972), 376–82. An annotated bibliographic survey of Greville scholarship through 1971.

CALDWELL, MARK L. "Sources and Analogues of the *Life of Sidney.*" *Studies in Philology*, 74 (1977), 279–300. Good for the political content and purposes of the *Life*.

ELLIS-FERMOR, UNA. "Fulke Greville." In *The Jacobean Drama*. 4th ed. London: Methuen, 1958, pp. 191–200. Judges Greville severely as a dramatist, but praises the weight and profundity of his themes.

FARMER, NORMAN K., JR. "Fulke Greville and the Poetic of Plain Style." *Texas Studies in Literature and Language*, 11 (1969), 657–70. Greville's views on the dangers of the undisciplined imagination led him to adopt a more limited style than that of his friend Sidney.

———. "Holograph Revisions in Two Poems by Fulke Greville." *English Literary Renaissance*, 4 (1974), 98–110. The process of creation in two *Caelica* lyrics as it affects the unity of the whole cycle.

JACQUOT, JEAN. "Religion et Raison d'Etat dans l'Oeuvre de Fulke Greville." *Etudes Anglaises*, 5 (1952), 211–22. Shows the tension in the dramas between religion and political power.

LEVY, F. J. "Fulke Greville: The Courtier as Philosophic Poet." *Modern Language Quarterly*, 33 (1972), 433–48. A review-essay of the biographies of Rebholz and Rees with some important original biographical considerations.

LITT, GARY R. " 'Images of Life': A Study of Narrative and Structure in Fulke Greville's *Caelica.*" *Studies in Philology*, 69 (1972), 217–230. An overview of the thematic progression of the cycle.

MACLEAN, HUGH N. "Fulke Greville: Kingship and Sovereignty." *Huntington Library Quarterly*, 16 (1953), 237–71. On the treatises, principally *Monarchy*, analyzing the historical and philosophical bases for Greville's theories of government.

———. "Fulke Greville on War." *Huntington Library Quarterly*, 21 (1958), 95–109. Examines Greville's pragmatic and religious defenses in the treatises for the existence of war.

MORRIS, IVOR. "The Tragic Vision of Fulke Greville." *Shakespeare Survey*, 14 (1966), 66–75. A discussion of the theory of tragedy implied by the choruses of Greville's two plays.

PETERSON, DOUGLAS. "Fulke Greville's *Caelica.*" In *The English Lyric from Wyatt to Donne: A History of the Plain and Eloquent Styles*. Princeton: Princeton University Press, 1967, pp. 252–84. A reading of *Caelica* in light of Yvor Winters' views on Greville as a "plain" stylist.

REBHOLZ, RONALD. "Love's Newfangleness: A Comparison of Greville and Wyatt." *Studies in the Literary Imagination*, 11(1978), 17–30. Examines the prevalence of the theme of infidelity in *Caelica* and Wyatt's lyrics.

ROBERTS, DAVID A. "Fulke Greville's Aesthetic Reconsidered." *Studies in*

Philology, 74 (1977), 388–405. Uses passages from the *Life of Sidney* and *Humane Learning* to adduce Greville's theory on the function of literature.

URE, PETER. "Fulke Greville's Dramatic Characters." *Review of English Studies*, n.s. 1 (1950), 308–23. Defends Greville as a dramatist, showing his adaptations of Senecan forms so as to highlight anguish in the inner lives of his characters.

WALLER, G. F. "Fulke Greville's Struggle with Calvinism." *Studia Neophilologica*, 44 (1972), 295–314. An analysis of those sections of the treatises that show Greville's general adherence to, and occasional divergences from, Calvinistic doctrines.

WEINER, ANDREW D. *Sir Philip Sidney and the Poetics of Protestantism: A Study of Contexts*. Minneapolis: University of Minnesota Press, 1978. Of the recent work on Sidney, the most relevant to Greville students.

WILKES, G. A. "The Sequence of the Writings of Fulke Greville, Lord Brooke." *Studies in Philology*, 56 (1959), 489–503. Presents a plausible sequential arrangement of the corpus, but attaches no specific dates.

WINTERS, YVOR, "The Sixteenth-Century Lyric in England." *Poetry*, 53 (1939), 258–72, 320–35; 54 (1939), 35–51. Revised and reprinted in *Forms of Discovery: Critical and Historical Essays on the Forms of the Short Poem in English*. Chicago: Alan Swallow, 1967, pp. 1–121. A crucial article in establishing Greville's importance as a poet of philosophical eminence and stylistic severity.

Index